FARMSTAND FAVORITES COOKBOOK

OVER 300 RECIPES

CELEBRATING LOCAL, FARM-FRESH FOOD

FOREWORD BY AVIS RICHARDS

PHOTOGRAPHS BY CATARINA ASTROM

Hatherleigh Press is committed to preserving and protecting the natural resources of the Earth. Environmentally responsible and sustainable practices are embraced within the company's mission statement.

Hatherleigh Press is a member of the Publishers Earth Alliance, committed to preserving and protecting the natural resources of the planet while developing a sustainable business model for the book publishing industry.

This book was edited and designed in the village of Hobart, New York. Hobart is a community that has embraced books and publishing as a component of its livelihood. There are several unique bookstores in the village. For more information, please visit www.hobartbookvillage.com.

DISCLAIMER
This book offers general cooking and eating suggestions for educational purposes only. In no case should it be a substitute nor replace a healthcare professional. Consult your healthcare professional to determine which foods are safe for you and to establish the right diet for your personal nutritional needs.

Library of Congress Cataloging-in-Publication Data is available upon request.
978-1-57826-420-9

All Hatherleigh Press titles are available for bulk purchase, special promotions, and premiums. For information about reselling and special purchase opportunities, please call 1-800-528-2550 and ask for the Special Sales Manager.

Interior Design by Nick Macagnone
Cover Design by Dede Cummings Designs
Photographs by Catarina Astrom

10 9 8 7 6 5 4 3 2 1

Printed in the United States

Improve your life. Change your world.

TABLE OF CONTENTS

FOREWORD
The Importance of Sustainable and Healthy Food
Avis Richards

Sustainable and healthy food has always been important to me. I believe it's one of the keys to a better lifestyle, as well as being vital to keeping our planet green for generations to come. For as long as I can remember, I've been enthusiastically sharing this passion with my family, friends, and the New York community. It's been a very rewarding experience for me, but there can never be too many voices supporting healthy eating, which is why it's a real joy seeing *The Farmstand Favorites Cookbook* come to fruition.

I've discovered that many people simply don't realize how easy it can be to make the switch to more sustainable and healthier options when it comes to eating. Everyday we're inundated with ads for products that have been processed and mass-produced, which are empty of any real nutritional value. We've fallen into a routine that can be tough to break free from. However, once you begin to make the right choices and seek out the healthy, more environmentally friendly alternatives, you'll begin to see just how easy it is and you'll quickly find yourself making new, better habits. Many of these options are available in the same grocery you visit each week, while others can be found at local farmers markets, sold by the very same people who grow or make them. The benefits of eating farm fresh foods extend beyond your dining room table and into your community. It supports local growers and businesses, and it means less energy is used in getting food from the farm to your table.

Choosing to eat farm fresh foods will open a new world of delectable culinary options. Hatherleigh Press' *Farmstand Favorites* series has quickly become a favorite in my kitchen, with each focusing on a specific ingredient. There are always new flavors to explore, and because farm fresh ingredients are the key to better food, just making the right choices will make you feel like a rock star in the kitchen. Whether I'm preparing a holiday dinner or just a quick meal for that one moment when the family comes together during a busy weekday, it's always delicious if I'm cooking with farm fresh ingredients.

I believe in sustainable food, but we have a lot of work ahead of us if we want a healthier, greener country. Choosing farm fresh produce, buying organic meat, and eating grassfed beef are just a few of the easy and enjoyable steps in the right direction. It gets us back to our roots. Even by doing something as simple as snacking on local produce instead of greasy potato chips, you'll be doing a favor for your body and the earth. Hatherleigh Press believes in this as much as I do and you can't go wrong with *The Farmstand Favorites Cookbook* as a guide to healthier, greener meals. Once you make the change to farm fresh foods, you'll never want to look back.

Avis Gold Richards is the founder and CEO of Birds Nest Foundation™, a 501(c)3 non-profit creative group that produces several television shows, documentaries, and short films for charitable organizations. Avis also launched "The Ground Up Campaign" a national campaign providing indoor edible academic gardens and curriculum to over 100 classrooms. Avis has produced and directed hundreds of episodes and films for national and local broadcast, websites, and events. Avis was recently nominated for three New York Emmy Awards and has won numerous Stevie, W3, Telly, Davey, and Aurora Awards for producing non-profit films and videos. Avis produced a public television series entitled "Lunch" for NYC Media, after the successful launch of her short documentary, "LUNCH," which was in support of Earth Day Network. Following these successes, she also produced over 40 episodes for the television show "Dylan's Lunchbox", which aired on NYC Media, Plum TV, and Taxi TV. Avis is currently producing the second season of "Dylan's Lunchbox", which will be aired on NYC Media starting this fall, and the documentary "Lunch 2: The Solutions", the sequel to "Lunch".

BREAKFAST

Morning dawns. Streaks of sunlight peek through your window, beckoning you to arise. You roll out of bed and commence with the morning ritual to prepare for the day that awaits you. Shower, shave, brush your teeth, dress, apply makeup, gather your items for the day, kiss the family goodbye, then grab a cup of coffee and something quick to eat as you hurry out the door. While your routine may be slightly different, the reality is the same for most everyone. Although experts have been proclaiming the importance of starting the day with a healthy, homemade breakfast for years, it is still the most commonly rushed meal of the day, and is sometimes even skipped altogether.

Much like your morning routine prepares you for the events of the coming day, so does eating a homemade and nutritious breakfast. In fact, it is even more important. Enjoying a breakfast rich in fresh fruits, vegetables, dairy, grains, and other natural ingredients provides your body with the proper fuel it needs and helps set the tone of your entire day.

Kick start your weekend mornings by relaxing on the front porch with a loved one and enjoy a cup of coffee or tea. Then move inside to enjoy a hearty breakfast of omelets and pancakes topped off with fresh fruit or pure maple syrup. On those weekdays when your schedule is more rushed and breakfast on-the-go is the only choice, opt to plan ahead and make your breakfast the evening before. Homemade muffins and breakfast squares that are made with fresh farmstand ingredients such as Strawberry-Blueberry Muffins (page 6) or Tomato, Cheddar, and Mushroom Breakfast Squares (page 15) serve as excellent choices for busy workday mornings, while still providing your body with delicious natural goodness.

Sweet Potato Pancakes with Apple-Walnut Topping

Ingredients:

6 cups sweet potatoes or yams, shredded
¼ cup all-purpose flour
½ teaspoon baking powder
¼ teaspoon ground cinnamon
1 tablespoon honey
1 large egg
2 large egg whites

½ cup light brown sugar, firmly packed
⅓ cup walnuts, chopped
1 tablespoon orange juice
½ teaspoon ground cinnamon
2 baking apples, peeled, cored, and thinly sliced (McIntosh or Cortland will work well)

Directions:

In a large bowl, combine sweet potatoes, flour, baking powder, cinnamon, honey, egg, and egg whites and stir with a fork until mixed well. Coat a large nonstick skillet with cooking spray and place over medium heat. Drop the batter by about 2 tablespoonfuls into hot pan to make several pancakes. Flatten slightly with a spatula until about 3 inches across. Cook the pancakes until golden on both sides. Transfer the pancakes to a warm large plate and keep warm. Repeat with the remaining batter, coating the skillet with cooking spray, as needed.

Topping

In a large skillet, stir together brown sugar, walnuts, orange juice, and cinnamon. Add the apples and cook over medium-high heat, stirring, until the apples are tender and the brown sugar has melted to form a syrup. Serve with the pancakes.

A THING OR TWO ABOUT APPLES

- Apples are grown in the continental U.S. and are commercially grown in 36 states.
- America's top apple producing states are Washington, New York, Virginia, California, Pennsylvania and Michigan.

Oatmeal Pancakes with Cranberries

Courtesy of the American Institute for Cancer Research

(www.aicr.org)

Ingredients:

½ cup all-purpose flour
¼ cup whole-wheat flour
¼ teaspoon salt
1 tablespoon sugar
½ teaspoon baking powder
¾ teaspoon baking soda
¾ cup quick-cooking (not instant) oats
2 egg whites, lightly beaten

1 cup plain low-fat yogurt
1 cup low-fat milk
1 teaspoon vanilla
2 tablespoons canola oil
½ cup dried cranberries
Powdered sugar (optional)
Juice of 1 lemon (optional)
Cooking spray

Directions:

Preheat the oven to 200°F. In a medium bowl, sift together all-purpose and whole-wheat flours. Add the remaining dry ingredients and mix well. In a separate bowl, beat the egg whites, yogurt, milk, vanilla, and oil. Add the wet ingredients to the dry ingredients, making sure not to over-mix. Stir in the cranberries. For the very best results, allow the batter to rest, covered, in the refrigerator for 30 minutes. Spray a griddle or large, flat pan with cooking spray. Heat to medium-high. Pour ¼ cup batter for each pancake and cook for approximately 2 to 3 minutes.

When bubbles appear on the upper surface, flip the pancakes. Continue cooking until the second side is golden brown, about 2 minutes. As you make more pancakes, keep the finished pancakes in the warmed oven on a cookie sheet, separated with parchment paper. When ready to serve, lightly dust pancakes with powdered sugar and a squeeze of fresh lemon juice.

Pancakes

Ingredients:

1 teaspoon baking powder
2 cups flour
4 eggs
1 teaspoon salt
2 cups milk

Directions:

Blend baking powder and flour in a small bowl. Separate egg whites from yolks, then beat the whites and yolks of eggs separately. Add the egg yolks, salt, egg whites, and half of the milk in a mixing bowl. Gradually add the flour mixture and the remainder of milk, alternating between the two until the batter is of the desired consistency. Grease the bottom of a hot frying pan, pour in a large ladleful of batter, and fry quickly. Serve with pure maple syrup.

Cornmeal Pancakes with Honey Fruit Sauce

Courtesy of the National Honey Board

(www.honey.com)

Makes 8 pancakes

Ingredients:

Fruit Sauce

1 cup orange juice

1 apple, pared, cored and diced

1 pear, pared, cored and diced

⅓ cup honey

1 teaspoon grated orange peel

1 tablespoon cornstarch

¼ cup water

Cornmeal Pancakes

½ cup flour

½ cup cornmeal

3 teaspoons baking powder

½ teaspoon salt

1 cup milk

1 egg

3 tablespoons honey

3 tablespoons butter or margarine, melted

Directions:

Fruit Sauce

Combine orange juice, apple, pear, honey and orange peel in medium saucepan. Bring mixture to boil, reduce heat, and simmer 8 to 10 minutes or until fruits are tender. Dissolve cornstarch in water. Stir into hot mixture; cook and stir until mixture comes to a boil; simmer 1 minute. Makes 2⅓ cups.

Cornmeal Pancakes

Combine flour, cornmeal, baking powder, and salt in medium bowl; mix well and set aside. Combine milk, egg, honey, and melted butter in small bowl; mix well. Pour liquid mixture into flour mixture; stir only until moistened (batter will be lumpy). Pour about ¼ cup batter for each pancake in hot skillet or on griddle over medium-low heat; cook until bubbles form on surface and edges become dry. Turn and cook 2 minutes longer or until golden. Serve with Fruit Sauce.

Pumpkin Pancakes

Ingredients:

1 cup cooked pumpkin

2 eggs

1½ pints milk

2 teaspoons baking powder

Salt

Flour (enough to make a good batter, about 2 cups)

Directions:

Mix together the cooked and cooled pumpkin, eggs, milk, baking powder, a little salt, and flour to make good batter. Beat until smooth and cook on the griddle.

Pumpkin Waffles with Blueberries and Pomegranate Coulis

Makes 8 waffles

Ingredients:

2 cups flour, sifted
4 tablespoons turbinado sugar (or light brown sugar)
1 tablespoon baking powder
1 teaspoon baking soda
¼ teaspoon salt

1 tablespoon pumpkin pie spice
2 extra-large eggs, separated
1¾ cups buttermilk
½ cup pumpkin puree
2 tablespoons melted butter
1¼ cup blueberry juice (no sugar added)
1¼ cup pomegranate juice (no sugar added)

Directions:

Place the juices and 1 tablespoon sugar in a pan. Bring to simmer over medium heat and reduce to 1 cup. Remove from heat and set aside to cool. Mix the flour, remaining 3 tablespoons sugar, baking powder, baking soda, salt, and pumpkin pie spice together in a large bowl. In another bowl, whisk the egg yolks and buttermilk until frothy. Blend in the pumpkin puree and melted butter. Pour the mixture over the dry ingredients and mix until incorporated. Whisk the egg whites until set and gently fold into the prepared mixture. Preheat a waffle iron, according to manufacturer's recommendations. Quickly spread batter to the rim and cook until the steaming stops and until the waffle is golden brown. Repeat with the remaining batter. Serve each waffle with 2 tablespoons of coulis.

Note: While making a large portion of waffles, you can keep them warm in a 270°F preheated oven.

Coulis is typically a thick fruit sauce, but in this recipe we are using a no-sugar-added juice as a healthier alternative.

Spiced Egg Nog French Toast

Courtesy of Garelick Farms
(www.garelickfarms.com)

Ingredients:

2 cups egg nog
½ teaspoon cinnamon
½ teaspoon nutmeg
¼ teaspoon cloves

2 eggs
12 slices firm (day-old) white bread
4 tablespoons butter or margarine

Directions:

Combine egg nog, spices, and eggs; beat with a wire whisk for 1-2 minutes. Melt butter or margarine in a non-stick skillet over medium heat. Dip slice of bread in egg mixture on each side. Fry egg-dipped bread in skillet over medium heat until golden brown on each side. Serve with maple syrup, honey or butter. Enjoy!

Honey French Toast

Ingredients:

2 eggs, slightly beaten
¼ cup honey
¼ cup milk
¼ teaspoon salt
6-8 slices bread

Directions:

Blend the eggs, honey, milk, and salt in a medium-sized mixing bowl. Dip a slice of bread in mixture, coat well, and fry on a greased (or buttered) griddle until it is golden brown. Serve French toast immediately with liquid honey, creamed honey, or butter.

Strawberry-Blueberry Muffins

Courtesy of the American Institute for Cancer Research

(www.aicr.org)

Ingredients:

3 tablespoons canola oil
⅓ cup unsweetened applesauce
½ cup sugar
2 eggs
1 teaspoon vanilla
1 cup fresh blueberries
1 cup chopped fresh strawberries
1 cup whole-wheat flour
1 cup unbleached all-purpose flour
2 teaspoons baking powder
¼ teaspoon salt
½ cup fat-free milk
Canola oil spray

Directions:

Preheat oven to 375°F. Spray 12-cup muffin tin with canola oil and set aside. In medium bowl, whisk together oil, applesauce, sugar, and eggs. Add vanilla, blueberries, and strawberries. In separate bowl, blend together flours, baking powder, and salt. Fold in half flour mixture, then half milk. Add remaining flour and milk, folding in just until blended. Scoop batter into prepared tins. Bake 25-30 minutes or until golden brown and inserted toothpick comes out dry. Allow muffins to cool for 20 minutes before removing from pan.

Honey Bran Muffins

Ingredients:

1 cup flour
½ teaspoon baking soda
½ teaspoon salt
2 cups bran
½ cup honey

1 tablespoon margarine, melted
1½ cups milk
¾ cup walnuts, chopped (optional)

Directions:

Sift together the flour, baking soda, and salt. Blend in the bran. Add the remaining ingredients and mix well. If walnuts are desired, stir them in at this time. Scoop mixture into greased muffin tins or paper liners. Bake at 375°F for approximately 30 minutes.

Maple Sour Cream Muffins

Courtesy of the New York State Maple Producers Association
(www.nysmaple.com)

Ingredients:

1¾ cups flour
1 teaspoon baking soda
2 teaspoons baking powder
½ teaspoon salt
½ cup butter
1¾ cups pure maple syrup
1 cup sour cream

1 egg
½ cup chopped pecans
Pure maple cream (optional)

Directions:

Preheat oven to 400°F. Grease a 16-cavity standard muffin pan. Stir together all dry ingredients (except pecans) and set aside. In another bowl, cream butter. Add maple syrup, sour cream, and egg. Stir in pecans. Add the dry ingredients and stir until blended. Spoon batter in pan about ⅔ full. Bake 15-17 minutes. Cool and remove from pan. Drizzle with maple cream if desired.

Harvest Pumpkin Muffins

Courtesy of the National Honey Board

(www.honey.com)

Makes 12 muffins

Ingredients:

1½ cups all-purpose flour

1½ teaspoons baking powder

1 teaspoon baking soda

¼ teaspoon salt

1½ teaspoons ground cinnamon

½ teaspoon ground ginger

¼ teaspoon ground nutmeg

¼ cup (½ stick) butter or margarine, softened

¾ cup honey

1 egg

1 cup solid packed pumpkin

1 cup chopped toasted walnuts

Directions:

In medium bowl, combine flour, baking powder, baking soda, salt, cinnamon, ginger, and nutmeg; set aside. Using an electric mixer, beat butter until light; beat in honey, egg, and pumpkin. Gradually add flour mixture, mixing until just blended; stir in walnuts. Spoon into 12 greased or paper-lined 2½-inch muffin cups. Bake at 350°F for 25 to 30 minutes, or until toothpick inserted in center comes out clean. Remove muffins from pan to wire rack. Serve warm or at room temperature.

Golden Apple Oatmeal

Ingredients:

1 Golden Delicious apple, diced

⅓ cup apple juice

⅓ cup water

Dash cinnamon

Dash nutmeg

⅓ cup quick-cook rolled oats, uncooked

Directions:

Combine apples, juice, water and spices; bring to a boil. Stir in rolled oats; cook 1 minute. Cover and let stand several minutes before serving.

Apple-Honey Oatmeal

Ingredients:
⅔ cup rolled oats
2 cups boiling water
½ teaspoon salt
6 medium-sized apples
1 cup water
¼ cup honey

Directions:
Stir the rolled oats into a pot of boiling water with ½ teaspoon salt and cook them until they thicken. Place the oats in a double boiler and cook for 2 to 4 hours. Pare, core, and slice the apples. Cook the apples in a syrup made of the water and honey until they are soft, but not soft enough to fall apart. To serve, put a large spoonful of the cooked oats in each dish and arrange apple slices on top of the oats. Pour a small amount of the syrup left from cooking the apples over the top and serve immediately.

Note: You may also speed up this process by using quick oats instead of rolled oats.

Banana-Oatmeal Breakfast Brulée

Courtesy of Garelick Farms
(www.garelickfarms.com)

Ingredients:
4 cups (1 quart) fat-free milk
2 cups quick-cooking rolled oats
¼ teaspoon salt
6 tablespoons brown sugar, divided use
1 cup low-fat French vanilla yogurt
2 bananas, thinly sliced

Directions:
Combine the milk, rolled oats, salt, and 2 tablespoons of the brown sugar in a large sauce-pan and mix well. Bring to a boil over medium heat. Continue to cook, stirring constantly for 1 minute. Spoon 1 cup of the oatmeal into each of four au gratin dishes or ovenproof bowls. Press the oatmeal down with the back of a spoon to spread it evenly over the bottom of the dish. Top each serving with ¼ cup of the yogurt, spreading it evenly over the entire surface. Arrange ½ of a sliced banana evenly over the top of each serving and then sprinkle each with 1 tablespoon of the remaining brown sugar. Arrange the dishes on a baking sheet or in a large baking pan and place under a preheated broiler until the sugar starts to bubble and turn dark, about 1 to 2 minutes. Serve immediately.

Maple Granola

Courtesy of the New York State Maple Producers Association

(www.nysmaple.com)

Ingredients:

3 cups old-fashioned rolled oats

½ cup sliced almonds

½ cup roasted cashews

½ cup roasted sesame seeds

½ cup roasted sunflower seeds

¼ cup unsalted butter

½ cup pure Grade B maple syrup

½ cup vegetable oil

½ teaspoon vanilla extract

¼ cup granulated pure maple sugar

1 cup raisins or dried cranberries

Directions:

Preheat oven to 325°F. In a large bowl, combine the oats, almonds, cashews, sesame seeds, and sunflower seeds. In a small saucepan, combine the butter, maple syrup, oil, vanilla, and maple sugar. Cook over medium heat for 5 minutes. Pour over the dry mixture and stir until well blended. Spread the mixture out on a baking sheet in an even layer. Bake, stirring occasionally, for about 30 minutes or until golden. Remove from the oven and let cool. Stir in the raisins or cranberries. Store in an airtight container at room temperature for up to 2 weeks.

Homemade Granola with Pumpkin Yogurt

Makes 10 (½ cup) servings

Ingredients:

Granola

¼ cup honey

¼ cup vegetable oil

2 teaspoons pumpkin pie spice

1 teaspoon almond extract

½ teaspoon orange extract

3½ cups old fashioned oats, uncooked

¼ cup sliced almonds

¼ cup chopped walnuts

Yogurt

½ cup low-fat yogurt

1 tablespoon pumpkin puree

Directions:

Preheat the oven to 350°F. In a bowl, mix the honey, oil, spice, and extracts. Stir in the oats and nuts. Mix ½ cup low-fat yogurt and 1 tablespoon pumpkin puree for every ½ cup of granola. Mix well and spread over a greased cookie sheet. Bake for 10 minutes. Stir and continue to bake for another 10 minutes or until golden brown. Cool completely and break apart.

Yogurt-Granola Parfait

Ingredients:
1¾ cups plain or vanilla yogurt
6 tablespoons honey
8 ounces fresh berries (blackberries, blueberries, raspberries and/or strawberries)
2 Cameo apples
2½ cups granola

Directions:
Stir together the yogurt and 4 tablespoons of the honey in a small bowl. Pick over the berries to remove any stems or leaves and halve or quarter larger berries. Put the berries in a medium bowl. Quarter and core the apples and cut them into ¼-inch dice.

Stir the apples and the remaining 2 tablespoons of honey into the berries. Spoon a few tablespoons of the granola into the bottom of each sundae dish or wine glass. Top the granola with a few tablespoons of yogurt, then add a generous spoonful of the apple-berry mixture. Repeat the layering one more time, drizzling any remaining juice from the fruit over the top.

Strawberry Omelet

Ingredients:
3 eggs
Pinch salt
2 tablespoons cold water
1 pint strawberries
3 tablespoons sugar

Directions:
Separate the whites and yolks of two eggs. Beat the whites to a stiff froth. Mix the yolks with a pinch of salt and the cold water. Pour the yolk mixture slowly into the beaten whites while beating constantly. Grease the bottom of a pan with non-stick spray or a small amount of butter. Pour in the eggs, cover, and cook for 3 minutes. Loosen the omelet; if it sticks in some places to the pan, slip a broad-bladed knife underneath the omelet, lift it up on the side it sticks, and slip a small piece of butter underneath it; as soon as the omelet is loose, cover it again, and cook it until you can touch the top with your finger without any of the omelet adhering to it, then fold it over and slip it onto a plate. Wash and drain the strawberries, mash them with a fork, and add 3 tablespoons of sugar. When the omelet is baked, put part of the strawberries over the omelet, and fold. Pour the remaining strawberries around it and serve.

Cheese Omelet

Ingredients:
2 eggs
Pinch of salt
Pinch of pepper
½ teaspoon finely chopped parsley
1 teaspoon grated Parmesan, or other cheese

Directions:
Whisk two eggs thoroughly. Mix salt, pepper, parsley, and Parmesan completely into the eggs. Put a piece of butter the size of an egg into the frying-pan. When it is hot, pour in the mixture, and stir it with a wooden spoon until it begins to set. Discontinue stirring, but shake the pan for a minute or so. When the egg is cooked, fold the omelet in two. When it is lightly browned, turn it on a hot dish. It should not be overdone, and the inside should be quite juicy. The frying process should take three minutes. If preferred, the cheese may be finely grated and sprinkled over the omelet after it is cooked, instead of mixed with it before.

Omelet with Garlic Greens

Courtesy of Peter McClusky, Toronto Garlic Festival
(www.torontogarlicfestival.ca)
Serves 1

Ingredients:
1 tablespoon unsalted butter
½ cup garlic greens, cut in half lengthwise and chopped crosswise (use the tender light-colored part of the greens)
2 eggs, beaten
¼ teaspoon kosher salt
½ teaspoon freshly ground black pepper
¼ cup mushrooms (such as shiitake or button), thinly sliced
¼ cup grated cheddar, American, or Swiss cheese

Directions:
Heat a non-stick or seasoned 6- to 9-inch pan to medium heat for 1 minute. Add butter (being careful not to let it burn). Add garlic greens and cook 3-5 minutes. Remove from pan and set aside. Mix salt and pepper with beaten eggs and add to pan. Cook until the top begins to set. Add the cooked garlic greens, mushroom, and cheese. If desired, place a lid on the pan to retain heat and help the top part of the omelet to cook. Starting from the edge of the pan, use a heat-proof spatula to fold one-third of the omelet toward the center of the pan and continue until the omelet is roll-shaped. Tilt the pan over a warmed serving plate until the omelet slides off the pan onto the plate. Serve with toast.

Tomato, Garlic, Crouton, and Pesto Omelet

Courtesy of the Florida Tomato Committee

(www.floridatomatoes.org)

Serves 1

Ingredients:

4 slices sturdy, white or whole-wheat bread

1 tablespoon olive oil

1 clove garlic, minced

2 large or extra-large eggs

1 teaspoon water

1 tablespoon unsalted butter

¼–⅓ cup grated mozzarella cheese

2 tablespoons homemade or store-bought pesto

1 large tomato, cut into bite-size chunks

Salt, to taste

Directions:

Preheat the oven to 300°F. Cut the bread into cubes and toss in a bowl with the oil and garlic. Spread the cubes on a baking sheet and toast them for 15 to 25 minutes, until golden brown. Transfer to a plate to cool. When you are ready to make the omelet, have all the ingredients nearby. Crack the eggs into a small bowl, add the water and salt, and beat lightly. Place a nonstick omelet pan over medium-high heat and add the butter. When it starts to sizzle, add the eggs. Stir the eggs with a fork in a circular motion. When the eggs start to set and form curds, spread them out evenly across the bottom of the pan. Immediately turn the heat to very low. Wait a few more seconds and, when the top layer of egg is almost entirely set, sprinkle the cheese over the surface. Dot the surface with the pesto. Scatter the tomatoes and a handful of the croutons over half of the omelet and fold the other half over the filled side. Slide the omelet out of the pan and serve at once. Serve with home fries or at dinner with a small serving of seafood.

Broccoli Frittata

Serves 4

Ingredients:

½ cup non-fat cottage cheese

8 eggs

1 large onion, diced

1 teaspoon olive oil

½ teaspoon dried dill

2 cups frozen chopped broccoli

2 teaspoons margarine

Directions:

Mix cottage cheese and eggs together; set aside. In large nonstick frying pan over medium heat, sauté onions in oil for 5 minutes, or until soft. Add dill and broccoli; sauté for 5 minutes, or until broccoli mixture softens. Set mixture aside. Wipe out frying pan. Add 1 teaspoon margarine and swirl the pan to distribute it. Add half of the vegetable mixture, and then add half of the egg mixture; lift and rotate pan so that eggs are evenly distributed. As eggs set around the edges, lift them to allow uncooked portions to flow underneath. Turn heat to low, cover the pan, and cook until top is set. Invert onto a serving plate and cut into wedges. Repeat with remaining 1 teaspoon margarine, vegetable mixture, and egg mixture.

Garlic Farmers' Boiled Egg with Minced Garlic

Courtesy of Peter McClusky, Toronto Garlic Festival

(www.torontogarlicfestival.ca)

Serves 1

Ingredients:

1 medium-sized egg

1 clove minced garlic

1 teaspoon unsalted butter

Salt (or veggie salt) and pepper, to taste

Directions:

Place the raw egg in a saucepan. Fill the saucepan with cool water to 1 inch above the egg. Cook over medium heat until the water starts to boil. Reduce heat and simmer for 2 to 3 minutes for soft-boiled consistency, five minutes for a medium-boiled egg, or 12 minutes for a hard-boiled egg. Remove the egg with a spoon and serve in an egg cup, small end down. Slice off the large end with a knife or egg scissors. Add garlic, butter, salt, and pepper and gently mix with egg yolk using a small spoon. Serve with toast.

Baked Eggs in Tomato Cups

Courtesy of Greensgrow Farm

(www.greensgrow.org)

Ingredients:

4 large tomatoes

1 cup grated Parmesan cheese, or less to taste

4 eggs

1 tablespoon fresh herbs such as oregano, basil, or sage

Salt and freshly ground pepper, to taste

Directions:

Preheat oven to 425°F. Slice tops off tomatoes, then scoop out seeds and pulp. Place tomatoes in a shallow baking dish and sprinkle cavities with salt, pepper, and a few pinches of cheese. Crack one egg into each tomato. Sprinkle with salt, pepper, herbs, and remaining cheese. Bake for 20 minutes for soft yolks or 30 to 35 minutes for hard yolks. Serve immediately.

Tomato, Cheddar, and Mushroom Breakfast Squares

Courtesy of the National Dairy Council

(www.nationaldairycouncil.org)

Ingredients:

2 teaspoons butter

2 cups sliced mushrooms

½ cup sliced green onion, including green tops

4 medium tomatoes

6 slices thick bread, cubed

2 cups shredded, reduced-fat cheddar cheese

2 cups fat-free low-fat milk

2 cups egg substitute

1 teaspoon hot pepper sauce

¼ teaspoon salt

Directions:

Preheat oven to 350°F. Spray an 8- x 8-inch square glass or ceramic baking dish with cooking spray; set aside. In a medium skillet over medium heat, melt the butter and add the mushrooms. Cook about 5 minutes or until mushrooms are softened and brown at the edges. Stir in green onion and tomatoes; set aside. Place half of the bread cubes in the prepared baking dish. Scatter half of the mushroom mixture and half of the cheese over the bread cubes. Layer the remaining bread cubes and mushroom mixture; set aside. In a large bowl, beat the milk, egg substitute, pepper sauce, and salt until well blended. Pour the milk mixture over the bread cubes and top with the remaining cheese. Cover the dish with foil and bake for 45 minutes. Remove foil and bake for an additional 15 minutes or until top is puffed up and cheese is browned at the edges. Let cool for 5 minutes, and then cut into squares to serve.

Make ahead suggestion: After assembling the recipe and covering with foil, you can refrigerate the ingredients for 8–10 hours before baking.

TOMATOES: TASTY AND HEALTHY

Research suggests that carotenoid lycopene found in tomatoes may reduce the risk for breast cancer. Because lycopene promotes bone health, studies have shown that lycopene also reduces the risk of osteoporosis.

Studies show that the antioxidant content of tomatoes supports bone, liver, kidney, cardiovascular, and bloodstream health. Due to their low calorie content, tomatoes are also linked with a lowered risk of obesity.

Cheese and Spinach Strudel
with Warm Tomato Relish

Courtesy of the Florida Tomato Committee

(www.floridatomatoes.org)

Serves 6

Ingredients:
Strudel

1 (10 oz.) package frozen chopped spinach

½ pound ricotta cheese

1 cup grated mozzarella cheese

⅔ cup freshly grated Parmesan cheese

2 pinches ground nutmeg

6 sheets phyllo dough, measuring 14- x 18-inches each

3 tablespoons unsalted butter

Fine dry bread crumbs

Salt and freshly ground pepper, to taste

Warm Tomato Relish

2 tablespoons olive oil

1 small onion, minced

1 celery rib, minced

4 large tomatoes, cored, seeded, and coarsely chopped

½ cup grated carrot

1 teaspoon fresh thyme or ½ teaspoon dried

1 teaspoon fresh lemon juice

2 teaspoons chopped fresh parsley

Salt and freshly ground pepper, to taste

Directions:
Strudel

Cook the spinach according to the package directions and cool on a plate. Squeeze out the excess moisture by hand and mix with the cheeses in a bowl. Stir in the nutmeg, salt, and pepper to taste. Preheat the oven to 375°F. To assemble, lay a sheet of phyllo on your work surface with a short edge facing you. Brush it lightly with butter and sprinkle with crumbs. Repeat this, layering until all the sheets of phyllo are used. About 3 inches from the short edge facing you, arrange the filling in a mounded row, about 3 inches wide, leaving about 3 inches uncovered along each long edge so that you can fold the sides over. Fold the sides of the phyllo over the filling and then fold the short end of exposed phyllo over the filling. Continue to roll the phyllo into a log. Poke two small steam vents in the top with a paring knife. Place the strudel on a baking sheet and bake for 30 to 40 minutes, until golden brown.

Warm Tomato Relish

While the strudel bakes, make the relish. Heat the oil in a medium-size nonreactive saucepan. Stir in the onion and celery and sauté over medium heat for 3 minutes. Stir in the tomatoes, carrot, thyme, and salt and pepper to taste. Simmer the relish gently until most of the liquid has cooked off. Remove from the heat. Right before serving, reheat the relish. Remove from heat and stir in the lemon juice and parsley. Slice the strudel and serve hot with some of the relish spooned around each slice.

Breakfast Tomatoes

Courtesy of Mariquita Farm

(www.mariquita.com)

Ingredients:

6 tomatoes, halved

Diced garlic, to taste

Olive oil, to taste

Salt and freshly ground pepper, to taste

Directions:

Sprinkle tomatoes with garlic and olive oil. Broil under the broiler until they are pleasantly browned. Season with salt and pepper to your liking. Serve with eggs or toast.

Note: These are a great way to get a vegetable serving into your first meal of the day.

Apple Soufflé

Ingredients:

1 pint steamed apples

1 tablespoon melted butter

½ cup sugar

Nutmeg, freshly grated

3 egg yolks

6 egg whites

Directions:

Stir the butter, sugar, nutmeg, and egg yolks into the steamed apples. Allow to cool. When this is cold, add the well-beaten whites to the mixture. Butter a 3-pint dish and turn the soufflé into it.

Bake thirty minutes in a hot oven. Serve immediately, with any kind of sauce.

Maple Sticky Buns

Courtesy of the New York State Maple Producers Association

(www.nysmaple.com)

Ingredients:

Dough

1⅓ cups water

¼ cup pure granulated maple sugar

1½ teaspoons salt

8 tablespoons butter

½ cup barley flour

2⅝ cups bread flour

½ cup dry milk

2½ teaspoons yeast

Filling

6 tablespoons butter, softened

1½ cups pure granulated maple sugar

4 teaspoons cinnamon

Topping

6 tablespoons melted butter

½ cup pure maple syrup

1 teaspoon cinnamon

Directions:

Dough

Place room temperature water in mixing bowl, then add remaining ingredients in order listed. Yeast should be added last in an indentation in the dry ingredients. Knead for approximately 5 minutes. When dough is finished, place on lightly floured board. Punch dough down and shape into an 8-inch wide rectangle (20 inches long).

Filling

Cream together the softened butter, maple sugar, and cinnamon to form a paste. Spread the filling evenly on the dough, and then roll.

Topping

Melt butter in a 9–x 13-inch baking pan. Mix with the syrup and cinnamon. Let stand until ready to put dough in the pan. Cut the dough roll into 16 slices and place on the syrup mixture in the baking pan. Cover and let rise about 45 minutes. Preheat oven to 375°F. Bake for 20-25 minutes. Invert to serve.

Breakfast Berry Corn Cakes

Ingredients:

½ cup corn meal
1 cup milk
½ cup sugar
1½ teaspoons baking powder
1 egg

1 tablespoon melted butter
½ cup fresh berries (raspberries, strawberries, blueberries, or cranberries will work best)
1 cup flour

Directions:

Mix together all ingredients, except for the flour. Pour into mini muffin tins. Using a fork, lightly sprinkle flour over the corn cakes. Bake at 400°F for approximately 20 minutes or until brown.

Pumpkin Butter on Toast

Ingredients:

1 (15 oz.) can pumpkin puree
Zest (large strips) of one orange
6 ounces freshly squeezed orange juice
1 tablespoon frozen orange concentrate
1 tablespoon pumpkin pie spices
Chopped pecans or walnuts, slightly toasted for stronger flavor
Whole-wheat bread slices, toasted

Directions:

Place the large strips of orange zest in a pan and cover with water. Bring to boil over high heat. Reduce heat and simmer for 10 minutes. Drain and mince the zest. Place the pumpkin puree, minced zest, orange juice, orange concentrate, and spices in a saucepan. Bring to boil over medium heat. Reduce heat and simmer for 20 minutes, stirring occasionally with a wooden spoon to avoid burning on the bottom. Check the flavor and adjust with more spices, if needed. Continue to cook until thickened. Remove from heat and cool. Transfer to a sanitized glass jar and refrigerate. Top one slice of toasted bread with pumpkin butter and toasted pecans or walnuts. Makes approximately 2 cups of pumpkin butter.

Note: For a fun afternoon snack, add some semi-sweet chocolate chips to the recipe.

SOUPS

Tasty garden favorites such as tomatoes, carrots, squash, potatoes, and onions that are grown in your own backyard or purchased at your local farmers market find their rightful place in a wide variety of soups and stews. Whether soup is offered as the main dish or a complementary dish, made with or without meat, comprised of fruit or vegetables, or served hot or cold, it is one type of food that simply never seems to go out of season, or out of demand.

There are few foods that are more soothing and satisfying on a chilly day than a nice big bowl of homemade soup or stew created with nutrient-rich vegetables and fruits plucked straight from the garden. When you or a loved one are feeling under the weather, enjoying a steaming serving of delicious and nutritious Chicken Vegetable Soup (page 22) does wonders to provide comfort and essential vitamins and minerals. Even on hot summer days, cold soup dishes like Scandinavian Fruit Soup (page 38) or Watermelon-Apple Gazpacho (page 37) can offer a healthy alternative for a chilled, refreshing treat as an afternoon snack or after-dinner dessert.

Soups and stews are also great choices to stretch meals from limited ingredients when your pantry supplies or finances are in a pinch, or if you find yourself with a houseful of guests to feed on a tight budget. Hearty soups, such as Irish Stew (page 40) or No-Peek Stew (page 32) offer satisfying and budget-friendly ways to serve a larger family or group of friends.

Chicken Vegetable Soup

Makes 4 quarts

Ingredients:

16 cups chicken broth
3 cups cooked chicken, chopped, or diced
1 cup onion diced
½ cup celery, diced
½ cup carrots, sliced
1 cup green beans
¼ cup parsley, chopped
1 teaspoon salt
Dash of pepper

Directions:

Combine all ingredients into a stainless steel saucepan and bring to a boil. Reduce heat and simmer for about an hour, or until vegetables are tender.

Prepare jars, lids, and pressure cooker according to manufacturer instructions.

Using a ladle and a funnel, spoon the hot soup into hot prepared jars, leaving 1 inch head space at the top of each jar.

Wipe the outer rim of the jars with a clean damp cloth to ensure a tight fit. Adjust the two-piece lids and secure snugly.

Place jars in prepared pressure cooker and process at 10 pounds pressure, or at 240°F (for pint jars, this will take 75 minutes and for quart jars it will take 90 minutes).

Note: Please read manufacturers' safety instructions regarding pressure cooking.

Chicken Gumbo

Makes 7 quarts

Ingredients:

4 pounds boneless chicken (thighs or breast), cut into 1-inch pieces
½ cup flour
1 teaspoon salt
½ teaspoon pepper
5 tablespoons lard
1 large onion, chopped
2 tablespoons parsley, chopped

3 tablespoons pimento, chopped
3 cups tomatoes, cored and quartered
4 cups water
2 teaspoons salt

Directions:

Coat chicken in flour, salt, and pepper. In a large frying pan, heat the lard. Brown the chicken in the hot lard and add onion. Brown onion lightly. In a large stainless steel saucepan, add browned chicken and onions with the remaining ingredients. Bring to a boil over medium-high heat and reduce heat, stirring occasionally. Cover and simmer for 1 hour.

Prepare jars, lids, and pressure cooker according to manufacturer instructions.

Using a ladle and a funnel, spoon the hot gumbo into hot prepared jars, leaving 1 inch head space at the top of each jar.

Wipe the outer rim of the jars with a clean damp cloth to ensure a tight fit. Adjust the two-piece lids and secure snugly.

Place jars in prepared pressure cooker and process at 10 pounds pressure, or at 240°F (for pint jars this will take 75 minutes and for quart jars it will take 90 minutes).

Serve over cooked rice.

TIPS FOR STORING CANNED PRODUCTS

Upon completion of any canning project, be sure to allow the product to cool for 24 hours. Once cooled, check each jar individually by pressing the middle of each lid to ensure the jar has sealed (if the jar has not sealed, you will be able to press the middle of the lid up and down). Discard the product of any jar that has not sealed properly. For those jars that have sealed properly, the seal will be concaved. Remove the outer band and wipe the processed jars. Label these and store in a cool, dry place.

SOUPS

Curried Butternut Apple Soup

Ingredients:

¼ cup reduced fat margarine

2 cups chopped onion

1 rib celery

4 teaspoons curry powder

2 medium butternut squash (about 2½-3 pounds) peeled, seeded, and cut into cubes

3 medium apples, peeled, cored, and chopped

3 cups water (or chicken stock or vegetable broth)

1 cup cider

Directions:

In a heavy kettle, combine margarine, onions, celery, and curry powder. Cover and cook over low heat until vegetables are tender (10-15 minutes), stirring often. Add cubed squash, chopped apples, and liquid (water, stock or broth) and bring to a boil. Reduce heat and simmer 20-30 minutes or until squash and apples are cooked thoroughly. Strain liquid and set aside. Purée the apple-squash mixture with one cup of the strained liquid. Add cider and remaining liquid to reach desired consistency. Garnish with grated apple, yogurt or low-fat sour cream.

Veal Scaloppini Soup

Makes 7 quarts

Ingredients:

3 pounds veal

6 tablespoons flour

2 teaspoons salt

½ teaspoon pepper

1 teaspoon paprika

5 tablespoons lard

2 garlic cloves, finely chopped

2 medium onions, sliced

1 teaspoon dry mustard

3 cups tomato juice

1 cup mushrooms, sliced

¼ cup parsley, chopped

Directions:

Cut veal into ½-inch slices. Mix flour, salt, pepper, and paprika in a bowl. Coat veal slices in flour and spice mix. In a large frying pan, heat the lard. Brown the veal in the hot lard. Add garlic and onions and brown lightly. In a large stainless steel saucepan place the veal and garlic and onion mixture, along with the dry mustard and tomato juice. Bring to a boil over medium-high heat and boil for 2 minutes. Reduce heat, cover, and simmer for 1 hour. Add mushrooms and parsley. Bring to a boil to heat thoroughly. Shut off the heat and cover.

Prepare jars, lids, and pressure cooker according to manufacturer instructions.

Using a ladle and a funnel, spoon the hot scaloppini into hot prepared jars, leaving 1 inch head space at the top of each jar.

Wipe the outer rim of the jars with a clean damp cloth to ensure a tight fit. Adjust the two-piece lids and secure snugly.

Place jars in prepared pressure cooker and process at 10 pounds pressure, or at 240°F (for pint jars this will take 75 minutes and for quart jars it will take 90 minutes).

Over the Moon Creamy Clam Chowder

Courtesy of Garelick Farms

(www.garelickfarms.com)

Ingredients:

6 ounces salt pork, trimmed and diced into ¼-inch pieces
3 tablespoons unsalted light butter
1½ cups coarsely chopped Vidalia onion
1 cup chopped celery
2 garlic cloves, minced
1½ pounds white potatoes peeled and diced into ½-inch pieces
4 (8 oz.) bottles clam juice
2 cups 1% low-fat milk
2 (15 oz.) cans cream-style corn
40 ounces canned, chopped clams, drained and juices reserved
1 teaspoon hot sauce
Chopped chives, to taste
Salt and pepper, to taste

Directions:

Stir salt pork in a 6-quart heavy pot over medium-low heat for about 15-20 minutes. Remove salt pork pieces, reserving fat. Add the butter, onions, celery, and garlic to the pot and sauté, stirring occasionally until the onions are softened and pale golden. Add potatoes and cover with bottled clam juice and reserved juice from canned clams (use added water if the stock does not cover potatoes). Bring to a boil, cover, and cook the potatoes until tender for about 15 minutes. Using a blender, puree low-fat milk and cream-style corn until completely smooth. Reduce the heat to low and gently stir in corn and milk mixture. Liberally season with salt and pepper to taste. Add clams, chives, and hot sauce and cook over low heat for 5 minutes, remove from heat and allow to sit for 15 minutes for flavors to blend. Enjoy with oyster crackers!

Note: All great chowders hail from New England! This creamy version features clams and milk. It's delicious served with oyster crackers.

Split Pea and Ham Soup

Makes 4 quarts

Ingredients:

2 (16 oz.) packages dried split peas
4 quarts water
3 cups carrots, sliced
1 large onion, chopped

2 cups ham, cooked and diced
2 teaspoons salt
1 teaspoon pepper

Directions:

Combine dried peas and water in a large stainless steel saucepan and bring to a boil over medium-high heat. Boil for 2 minutes, stir, and reduce heat. Cover and simmer for 1 hour, stirring occasionally. Add remaining ingredients and simmer for about 30 minutes, or until carrots are tender.

Prepare jars, lids, and pressure cooker according to manufacturer instructions.

Using a ladle and a funnel, spoon the hot soup into hot prepared jars, leaving 1 inch head space at the top of each jar.

Wipe the outer rim of the jars with a clean damp cloth to ensure a tight fit. Adjust the two-piece lids and secure snugly.

Place jars in prepared pressure cooker and process at 10 pounds pressure, or at 240°F (for pint jars this will take 75 minutes and for quart jars it will take 90 minutes).

Garlic Bean Soup

Serves 8

Ingredients:

1 pound dry Great Northern beans
1 quart water
1 quart low-sodium vegetable broth
3 tablespoons olive oil
2 garlic cloves, minced
4 tablespoons chopped parsley

Directions:

Place beans in large soup pot, cover with water and bring to boil. Cook 2 minutes, remove from heat. Cover pot and allow to stand for 1 hour. Drain, discarding the water. Combine beans, 1 quart fresh water, and vegetable broth in slow cooker. Sauté garlic and parsley in olive oil in skillet. Stir into slow cooker. Cover and cook on low for 8-10 hours or until beans are tender.

Creamy Squash Soup with Shredded Apples

Courtesy of NHLBI, part of NIH and HHS

Ingredients:

32 ounces puréed winter (butternut) squash
2 medium apples (try Golden Delicious or Gala)
1 tablespoon olive oil
½ teaspoon pumpkin pie spice
2 (12 oz.) cans fat-free evaporated milk

¼ teaspoon salt
⅛ teaspoon ground black pepper

Directions:

Peel then shred the apples using a grater or food processor, or peel and finely chop apples into thin strips. Set aside ¼ cup. Warm oil in a 4-quart saucepan over medium heat. Add all but ¼ cup of the apples. Cook and stir until apples soften, about 5 minutes. Stir in squash and pumpkin pie spice. Add the evaporated milk about ½ cup at a time, stirring after each addition.

Season with salt and pepper. Cook and stir over high heat just until soup is about to boil. Ladle into individual soup bowls. Top each with a tablespoon of the unused apples. Sprinkle with additional pumpkin pie spice, if desired.

Chayote Squash Soup with Cilantro Sour Cream

Serves 6

Ingredients:

1 large onion, chopped
2 garlic cloves, minced
1 tablespoon fresh ginger, minced
4 tablespoons flour
1 medium yellow pepper, sliced
3 large chayote squash, peeled, pitted, sliced
6 cups vegetable broth, divided

½ cup water
Cilantro, coarsely chopped, for garnish
Cooking spray

Cilantro Sour Cream
⅓ cup fat-free sour cream
1 tablespoon finely chopped cilantro
⅓ cup skim milk

Directions:

Spray large saucepan with cooking spray; heat over medium heat until hot. Sauté onion and garlic until tender; about 5 minutes. Stir in ginger and flour and cook over medium heat for 2 minutes, stirring constantly. Add pepper, squash, and 2 cups broth to saucepan; heat to boiling. Reduce heat to simmer until squash is tender, 15 to 20 minutes. Process mixture in food processor or blender until smooth; return to saucepan. Add remaining broth and water while continuing to heat; serve warm or cool to serve chilled. Drizzle with Cilantro Sour Cream and sprinkle of cilantro.

Roasted Acorn Squash and Apple Soup

Courtesy of the New York State Maple Producers Association

(www.nysmaple.com)

Ingredients:

1 medium acorn squash, quartered, seeds removed (see note below)

1 cup onions, peeled and diced

1 cup carrots, peeled and diced

1 cup celery, diced

3 apples (such as Cortland or McIntosh), peeled, cored and diced small

3 cloves garlic, minced

2 cups sherry wine

1 quart low-sodium chicken stock or chicken broth

1 cup heavy cream

1 cup pure maple syrup

Cider vinegar, to taste

Pure maple sugar, for garnish

Oil, as needed

Salt and pepper, to taste

Directions:

Place the acorn squash quarters on an oiled sheet tray, drizzle squash with oil and sprinkle with salt and pepper. Cover the entire tray with foil and bake in a 425°F oven for about 30 minutes or until starting to turn tender. Remove foil and bake an additional 30 minutes or until fork tender. Remove from oven. When cool enough to handle, scoop out flesh from squash skin. Discard skins. Heat a skillet over high heat until hot. Add enough oil to lightly coat the bottom of the pan and sauté the onions, carrots and celery until onions are translucent and caramelized. Add the apples and garlic and sauté 1-2 minutes more. Add the sherry wine and bring to a boil. Reduce by half. Add stock and bring to a boil. Let mixture simmer until apples and carrots are very tender, about 20 minutes. Add roasted squash. Finish with heavy cream, maple syrup, salt and pepper to taste. For flavor enhancement, add a splash of cider vinegar to the soup and stir well. Puree the soup with a stick blender, regular blender, or in a high-quality food processor until very smooth. Ladle soup into baked warm bowls and sprinkle with maple sugar before serving.

Note: If desired, wash the acorn squash seeds under cold water, sprinkle with salt, then spread on a sheet tray and roast in a 275°F oven until dried and crispy, about 40-50 minutes. Serve atop soup with maple sugar.

Winter Vegetable Soup
Serves 6

Ingredients:

1 cup chopped onions
1 sweet potato
2 carrots
1 pound banana or Hubbard squash
1 cup parsnips
2 cloves garlic
1 red bell pepper

2 cups low-sodium, low-fat vegetable broth
1 cup pureed tomato
2 tablespoons lime juice
¼ teaspoon cayenne
1 (10 oz.) package frozen peas
⅛ teaspoon black pepper
1 bunch cilantro sprigs, rinsed or thinly sliced green onions

Directions:

Peel onions and cut into ½-inch-thick wedges. Peel the sweet potato, carrots, squash, and parsnips; cut into ¾-inch pieces. Peel and mince or press garlic. Rinse bell pepper; stem, seed, and cut into ½-inch strips. Cook onions, sweet potato, carrots, squash, parsnips, garlic, and 1 cup of broth in a covered pan for 10 minutes, stirring occasionally. Add a few tablespoons of water if mixture begins sticking to pan. Add 1 more cup of broth, along with the bell pepper, tomato sauce, lime juice, and cayenne to taste. Return to a boil, and then reduce heat. Simmer, covered, until vegetables are tender when pierced, about 12 to 15 minutes. If stew sticks to pan or gets thicker than desired, add more broth as needed. Add peas and stir occasionally until hot, about 2 minutes. Add salt and pepper to taste. Ladle into soup bowls, and garnish with cilantro or sliced green onions.

THE HISTORY OF GARLIC

- The earliest documented use of garlic as a medicinal herb is from ancient Egypt.
- Believed to increase physical strength, garlic was eaten by ancient Greek warriors before battle.
- While constructing the ancient pyramids, slaves ate garlic to increase their endurance.

Pesto Minestrone

Serves 8

Ingredients:

Minestrone

2 cups coarsely chopped cauliflower (the equivalent of about 2 small heads)
1½ cups chopped zucchini (1-2 medium)
3 (14.5 oz.) cans low-sodium chicken broth
1 (16 oz.) can diced tomatoes, drained
1 cup uncooked elbow macaroni or small pasta shells
3 cups kidney beans or black-eyed peas, drained and rinsed
1 cup sliced carrot
1 cup chopped onion

Pesto

2 tablespoons olive oil
2 garlic cloves
1 cup fresh, loosely packed basil leaves
1 tablespoon water

Directions:

Minestrone

In a 5-6 quart saucepan, bring ½ cup water to boil and add tomatoes, cauliflower, onion and carrots; reduce heat and simmer, covered, 10 minutes or until vegetables are tender. Add zucchini, beans, broth, and pasta. Return to a boil, reduce heat, and simmer, uncovered, 10 minutes.

Pesto

Put all pesto ingredients in food processor or blender and process until very finely chopped. Just before serving, remove soup from heat and stir in pesto.

Hearty Pumpkin Soup

Ingredients:

3 pounds pumpkin
1 teaspoon olive oil
2 large onions, sliced (about 1 pound)
1 garlic clove, minced
6 cups gluten-free chicken stock
2 cups low-fat milk
2 fresh sage leaves
1 teaspoon freshly minced thyme
3 tablespoons low-fat Greek yogurt
2 tablespoons pumpkin seeds
Salt and pepper, to taste

Directions:

Peel the pumpkin and cut the flesh into medium cubes. Heat the oil in a large pan over high heat. Add the onions and sauté until translucent. Add the pumpkin, garlic, stock, milk, sage, and thyme, and bring to a boil. Reduce heat, cover, and simmer for 30 minutes. Puree the vegetables in a blender using just enough cooking liquid to obtain a creamy consistency. Return to the pan and season with salt and pepper. Stir in the yogurt, garnish with the pumpkin seeds, and serve immediately.

Pumpkin Curry Soup

Ingredients:

1 tablespoon butter
1 cup finely chopped onion
1 cup diced celery
2 garlic cloves, finely chopped
1 teaspoon curry powder
⅛ teaspoon ground coriander
⅛ teaspoon crushed red pepper

3 cups water
1 cup low-sodium chicken broth
32 ounces fresh pumpkin puree
1 cup fat-free half-and-half
Sour cream, for garnish
Chives, for garnish

Directions:

Melt butter in large saucepan over medium-high heat. Add onion, celery, and garlic; cook for 3 to 5 minutes or until tender. Stir in curry powder, coriander and crushed red pepper; cook for 1 minute. Add water and broth; bring to a boil. Reduce heat to low; cook, stirring occasionally, for 15 to 20 minutes to develop flavors. Stir in pumpkin and half-and-half; cook for 5 minutes or until heated through. Transfer mixture to food processor or blender (in batches, if necessary); cover. Blend until creamy. Serve warm or reheat to desired temperature. Garnish with dollop of sour cream and chives.

Tip: Soup may be prepared the day ahead. Cool to room temperature after adding pumpkin and half-and-half. Cover and refrigerate. Just before serving, blend then reheat to serving temperature, but do not boil.

Pumpkin Pistachio Soup

Ingredients:

1 small, fresh red chili
3 tablespoons sugar
1¼ cups whole, shelled California pistachios
1½ pounds seeded fresh pumpkin
2 shallots
2 stalks lemongrass (available in large supermarkets or Asian specialty stores)

1 tablespoon butter or margarine
3 cups vegetable stock
¼ teaspoon ground white pepper
¼ teaspoon ground cloves
6 tablespoons light sour cream or crème fraîche
Fresh cilantro

Directions:

Seed and finely chop chili. Melt sugar in skillet until it is a light brown caramel color. Add chili and pistachios and stir to coat. Turn mixture out of pan onto foil or wax paper and let cool. Pare pumpkin and cut into cubes. Peel and chop shallots. Cut lemon grass into 4-inch lengths. Melt butter in large saucepan, add shallots and lemon grass, cover and cook 1 minute. Add cubed pumpkin, stock, pepper and cloves. Cover and simmer over low heat for 15 to 20 minutes or until tender. Discard lemon grass. Puree pumpkin mixture in food processor or electric blender. Return to saucepan. Whisk in sour cream, heat gently then pour into wide soup bowls. Top with cilantro and caramelized pistachios.

No-Peek Stew

Courtesy of the American Beekeeping Federation (ABF)

(www.abfnet.org)

Ingredients:

2 pounds cubed beef
4-5 cubed raw potatoes
6 sliced raw carrots
2 stalks sliced or diced celery
1 onion, chopped
3 teaspoons instant tapioca

1½ teaspoons honey
1 teaspoon salt
¼ teaspoon black pepper
¼ teaspoon garlic salt (optional)
1½ cups tomato juice

Directions:

Put meat in a 9- x 13-inch baking pan. On top of the meat, place potatoes, carrots, celery, and onion. Mix remainder of ingredients and pour over all. Seal with foil and bake at 250°F for 5 hours. Do not peek!

Roasted Garlic Soup with Thyme Croutons

Courtesy of Hood River Garlic Farm

(www.hoodrivergarlic.com)

Serves 4

Ingredients:

Soup
4 heads organic garlic
3 cups milk
1 cup cream
Fresh thyme, to taste
Salt and pepper, to taste
Extra-virgin olive oil, to taste

Croutons
1 small loaf French bread
Fresh thyme, to taste
Salt and pepper, to taste
Extra-virgin olive oil, to taste

Directions:

Soup

Coat the garlic with olive oil, salt, and pepper and roast in a 350°F oven until the cloves are golden brown, about 45 minutes. Once the garlic is roasted, cut the head in half (from side to side), exposing all the cloves. Squeeze both halves into a bowl, discarding any skin. Pick out any fiber from the skin. Bring the roasted garlic, milk, cream, and thyme to a simmer. Simmer for 10 minutes. Puree in a blender, and then strain through a very fine mesh sieve. Season with salt and pepper. Serve with thyme, croutons, and a light drizzle of extra-virgin olive oil.

Croutons

Pre-heat the oven to 350°F. Remove the crust from the bread with a knife. Cut the loaf into very small cubes. Toss the cubes with a small amount of olive oil, fresh chopped thyme, salt, and pepper. Place the cubes on a tray and bake until golden brown, stirring occasionally. Serve while warm.

Flu Fighter Garlic Soup

Courtesy of Peter McClusky, Toronto Garlic Festival

(www.torontogarlicfestival.ca)

Serves 2

Ingredients:

2 tablespoons extra-virgin olive oil
1 medium or large onion, chopped
½ cup carrot, finely chopped
3 cups water or soup stock (either chicken stock or vegetable stock)
2 tablespoons roast garlic puree
4 minced garlic cloves

2 tablespoons chopped fresh parsley
¼ cup chopped fresh shiitake mushroom
1 teaspoon thyme
½ cup lentils
Kosher salt and freshly ground black pepper, to taste

Directions:

Add oil to medium-sized saucepan, set to medium heat. Add onions, stirring from time to time. Cook to a deep golden brown color. Add carrots, soup stock (or water), garlic puree, two of the garlic cloves, parsley, mushroom, thyme, lentils, salt, and pepper. Simmer for one hour. One minute before serving, add the two remaining garlic cloves. Serve in mugs or bowls.

Sweet and Hot Red Pepper and Tomato Soup

Courtesy of the National Honey Board

(www.honey.com)

Ingredients:

3 tablespoons vegetable oil
2 leeks, white part only, cleaned and chopped
1 stalk celery, chopped
2 medium red bell peppers, seeded and chopped
1 tablespoon grated fresh ginger root
1 (28 oz.) can plum tomatoes, chopped, reserve juice

3 cups chicken or vegetable broth
6 tablespoons honey
2 tablespoons balsamic vinegar
3 tablespoons fresh mint, chopped
3 tablespoons fresh parsley, chopped
Cayenne pepper, to taste
Salt and pepper, to taste

Directions:

In a large saucepan, heat oil over medium heat until hot. Add leeks, celery, and peppers; cook 8 to 10 minutes or until soft. Stir in cayenne and ginger; cook 1 minute. Stir in tomatoes with juice, broth, honey, and vinegar. Bring to a boil; reduce heat and simmer, partially covered, 25 minutes. Remove from heat. Cool soup slightly; puree in blender or food processor until smooth. Season with salt and pepper. Reheat if necessary and serve sprinkled with mint and parsley. Serve warm or cold.

Deluxe Cream of Tomato Soup

Courtesy of the Florida Tomato Committee
(www.floridatomatoes.org)
Serves 4–6

Ingredients:

2 tablespoons unsalted butter
1 small onion, finely chopped
2 celery ribs, finely chopped
4 large tomatoes, peeled, cored, seeded, and chopped (see note)
1 teaspoon sugar
2 cups chicken broth
½ cup heavy cream
2 teaspoons chopped fresh dill weed or 1 teaspoon dried
Salt and freshly ground pepper, to taste

Directions:

Melt the butter in a medium-size nonreactive saucepan. Add the onion and celery and sauté gently over medium heat for 5 minutes, stirring often; do not brown. Stir in the tomatoes and sugar. Simmer, covered, for 6 to 8 minutes until the tomatoes are soft. Transfer the vegetables to a food processor and process to a smooth puree. Pour the puree back into the saucepan and stir in the remaining ingredients. Heat the soup through, adjusting the seasoning as desired. Serve hot. Round it out with grilled cheese sandwiches, potato chips, and pickles, and you've got the makings for a surefire family favorite.

Note: To peel the tomatoes, submerge them for 15 to 30 seconds in boiling water. Remove to a colander and rinse briefly under cold water. The skins will slip right off.

THE HISTORY OF TOMATOES

Italy was the first European country to embrace the tomato. In Italian, tomatoes are called pomi d'oro, meaning "golden apples." The French believed that the tomato had aphrodisiac powers and named it pommes d'amour, which translates as "love apples." Thanks to its versatility, the tomato is now popular in a variety of cuisines. Today, approximately 130 million tons of tomatoes are produced each year, with the United States as one of the top three producers.

Roasted Tomato Soup

Courtesy of the Central New York Tomatofest, from the kitchen of Nadine Vande Walker
(www.cnytomatofest.org)

Serves 5–6

Ingredients:

6–7 medium tomatoes
½ medium red onion
3 tablespoons olive oil
2 teaspoons kosher salt
1 teaspoon sugar
1 teaspoon ground pepper

1 (14½ oz.) can chicken stock
1 cup light cream
2 tablespoons sugar
1 tablespoon fresh sliced basil
Salt, to taste
Sour cream, for garnish (optional)

Directions:

Preheat oven to 425°F. Cut tomatoes into quarters and spread out on a cookie sheet with the onions. Drizzle with oil. Sprinkle salt, sugar, and pepper on top. Roast the tomatoes for 30-40 minutes until the tomatoes and onions are tender and a little brown around the edges. Pour the tomatoes, onions, and juices into a saucepan. Add chicken stock, light cream, sugar, basil, and additional salt to the tomato mixture. Simmer for 30 minutes. Use a hand blender to puree until smooth. Serve with a little dollop of sour cream (optional).

Pepper and Tomato Stew

Courtesy of the Central New York Tomatofest, from the kitchen of Jason G. Wittwer
(www.cnytomatofest.org)

Ingredients:

1 green pepper, chopped
1 red pepper, chopped
1 medium white onion, diced
2 large tomatoes, diced and chopped
2 cups stewed tomatoes
1 pound lean ground turkey
1 pound ground Italian sausage (mild)

1 teaspoon Frank's® Red Hot sauce
1 teaspoon garlic powder
Salt and pepper, to taste
Fresh basil, for garnish

Directions:

Sauté the green pepper, red pepper, and onion in a medium pan over medium heat. Set aside in a 2-quart saucepan. Add the chopped tomatoes and stewed tomatoes. In a skillet, brown the ground turkey. When the turkey is browned, add to the saucepan. In the same skillet, brown the sausage. When the sausage is browned, add it to the saucepan. Place saucepan over low heat and simmer for 30 minutes or more. Add the hot sauce, garlic powder, salt, and pepper. Serve in a bowl. Garnish with fresh basil. Serve with garlic bread or crackers.

Note: A crock pot may be used in place of the 2-quart saucepan.

Fire-Roasted Tomato Gumbo

Courtesy of the Florida Tomato Committee

(www.floridatomatoes.org)

Serves 6

Ingredients:

5 large fully ripened fresh tomatoes (about
2½ pounds)

2 tablespoons butter

½ cup coarsely chopped Andouille sausage

½ cup coarsely chopped onion

½ cup coarsely chopped carrot

⅓ cup coarsely chopped celery

2 teaspoons finely chopped garlic

3 tablespoons all-purpose flour

3 cups chicken stock

3 tablespoons tomato paste

2 teaspoons sugar

1 teaspoon chopped fresh rosemary

½ teaspoon salt

¼–½ teaspoon ground red pepper (cayenne),
optional

¼ teaspoon ground white pepper

1 cup cooked white rice

¼ cup heavy cream

Croutons and rosemary sprigs, for garnish
(optional)

Directions:

Set a grill or broiler rack about 4 inches from the heat source; preheat the grill or broiler.
Core the tomatoes and place on the grill or in the roasting pan under the broiler. Cook,
turning once, until the skin blackens (30 to 40 minutes). In a medium saucepan, melt the
butter; add the sausage, onion, carrot, celery, and garlic. Cook, stirring occasionally, until
the vegetables just begin to brown (about 5 minutes); reduce heat to low. Sprinkle flour over
the vegetables; cook and stir until flour begins to brown (3 to 5 minutes). In a blender or
food processor, coarsely chop the grilled tomatoes; add the tomatoes to the vegetables in
the saucepan. Stir in the stock, tomato paste, sugar, rosemary, salt, red pepper, and white
pepper. Simmer, partially covered, for 15 minutes. Add rice and cream, then cook just until
hot. Spoon into soup plates dividing equally. Garnish with croutons and rosemary sprigs, if
desired.

"For to the bee a flower is a fountain of life, and to the flower a bee is a
messenger of Love."
—Khalil Gibran

Watermelon-Apple Gazpacho

Ingredients:

6 cups watermelon, seeded and cubed
1½ cups (2 medium) Golden Delicious apples, cored and chopped
½ cup (1 medium) onion, finely chopped
½ cup green bell pepper, finely chopped
1 teaspoon dried basil
½ teaspoon salt
¼ teaspoon black pepper, coarsely ground
¼ teaspoon chili powder
1 tablespoon cider vinegar

Directions:

In a blender, purée the watermelon until smooth; pour into a large bowl. Stir in the remaining ingredients. Cover and refrigerate at least 2 hours, or until well chilled.

Curried Date Carrot Soup
Serves 4

Ingredients:

⅔ cup pitted dates
1 onion, chopped
2 stalks celery, chopped
2 cloves garlic, minced
1 tablespoon ginger root, minced or substitute 1 teaspoon ground ginger
1½ tablespoons olive oil
2 tablespoons flour
2 (14 oz.) cans low-sodium chicken broth
2½ cups sliced carrots
1 teaspoon ground cumin
½ teaspoon curry powder
1 pinch cayenne pepper
1 pinch black pepper
1 tablespoon lemon juice

Directions:

Chop dates and set aside. In a heavy saucepan, sauté onions, celery, garlic, and ginger in oil over medium heat for 3–4 minutes or until translucent. Remove from heat and stir in flour. Return to heat and cook for 1–2 minutes, then whisk in chicken broth. Stir in carrots, cumin, curry powder, cayenne, and black pepper. Bring to a boil, reduce heat, cover and simmer 10 minutes, stirring occasionally. Stir in dates and simmer another 5–10 minutes, or until carrots are soft. Remove from heat and purée in a blender or food processor until smooth. Pour back into pan. Stir in lemon juice and return to stove top until thoroughly heated. Spoon into bowls and garnish with a spoonful of yogurt.

Maple and Parsnip Soup

Courtesy of the New York State Maple Producers Association

(www.nysmaple.com)

Ingredients:

3 pounds parsnips, peeled and sliced ¼-inch thick

1 large white onion, peeled and sliced ¼-inch thick

8 cups water

1 cup pure maple syrup

1 large bay leaf

1 cup heavy cream

Salt and white pepper, to taste

Directions:

Lightly brown parsnips and onions with vegetable oil in sauce pan, season lightly with salt and white pepper. Add water, maple syrup, bay leaf, and cover. Keep flame low and simmer until tender. Pull out bay leaf and puree all remaining ingredients in a food processor until smooth. Pour ingredients back into pot, add heavy cream, and reheat, being careful not to boil. Season to taste with salt and white pepper. Drizzle with maple syrup and serve warm with crusty bread.

Scandinavian Fruit Soup

Ingredients:

1 cup dried apricots

1 cup dried sliced apples

1 cup dried pitted prunes

1 cup dried cranberries

1 cup canned pitted red cherries

½ cup quick cooking tapioca

1 cup grape juice

3 cups water

½ cup orange juice

¼ cup lemon juice

1 tablespoon orange peel, grated

½ cup brown sugar

Directions:

Combine all dried fruits, cherries, tapioca, grape juice, and water in a slow cooker. Cover and cook on low for 8 hours. Before serving, stir in orange and lemon juices, orange peel, and brown sugar. Serve warm as soup or dessert. Serve chilled with vanilla frozen yogurt.

Apple Fennel Soup

Ingredients:

2 cups low-sodium chicken broth
2 cups water
½ cup white wine
2 Golden Delicious apples, peeled, cored and chopped
1 cup thinly sliced carrots
1 small onion, thinly sliced
1 cup chopped fennel
1 bay leaf
¼ teaspoon dried thyme leaves
6 peppercorns
4 teaspoons non-fat plain yogurt

Directions:

In large pot, combine all ingredients (except yogurt); bring to boil. Reduce heat and simmer, covered, 20 minutes. Strain soup, reserving liquid. Remove bay leaf from apple-vegetable mixture in strainer.

In blender or food processor, purée mixture; add reserved liquid and blend well. Reheat soup, if necessary, ladle into soup bowls and serve with a dollop of yogurt if desired.

Fruit Soup

Courtesy of Bees-And-Beekeeping.com

Ingredients:

3 pears
3 apples
4 cups water
1 tablespoon granulated tapioca
Juice from ½ lemon
⅛ teaspoon cinnamon
3 tablespoons honey

Directions:

Chop the pears and apples. Heat the water until boiling, then add the fruit and cook until tender. Press through a sieve, then add the tapioca and continue cooking until clear. Stir in the lemon juice, cinnamon, and honey. Serve either warm or as a cold fruit soup.

Irish Stew

Makes 7 quarts

Ingredients:

3 pounds lamb shank, cut into 2-inch pieces
4 tablespoons lard
2 cups water
2 teaspoons salt
1 teaspoon pepper
1 teaspoon paprika
¼ cup parsley, chopped
2 teaspoons celery seeds
1 large onion, chopped
2 cups turnips, diced
2 cups carrots, sliced
2 cups potatoes, diced
2 cups parsnips, diced

Directions:

In a large frying pan, brown the meat in hot lard. Place this in a large stainless steel saucepan, along with water, salt, pepper, paprika, parsley, and celery seeds. Bring to a boil over medium-high heat. Reduce heat and simmer, covered, for about 40 minutes, stirring occasionally. Add remaining ingredients and bring to a boil for 2 minutes. Reduce heat and simmer for 30 minutes, covered, stirring occasionally.

Prepare jars, lids, and pressure cooker according to manufacturer instructions.

Using a ladle and a funnel, spoon the hot stew into hot prepared jars, leaving 1 inch head space at the top of each jar.

Wipe the outer rim of the jars with a clean damp cloth to ensure a tight fit. Adjust the two-piece lids and secure snugly.

Place jars in prepared pressure cooker and process at 10 pounds pressure, or at 240°F (for pint jars this will take 75 minutes and for quart jars it will take 90 minutes).

Lentil Soup

Makes 7 quarts

Ingredients:

2 cups lentils, dry and uncooked
2 quarts water plus more to soak lentils
2 leek stalks, diced
2 tablespoons onion, chopped
2 cups celery, diced
2 cups carrots, diced

2 teaspoons salt
4 tablespoons bacon fat or lard
4 hot dogs, cut into ½-inch slices
2 tablespoons flour
1 tablespoon water

Directions:

In a large bowl, cover lentils with water and let these soak overnight. Drain the lentils. Place all ingredients (except flour and 1 tablespoon of water) in a large stainless steel saucepan and bring to a boil. Reduce heat and simmer for about an hour or until the carrots are tender.

Mix flour with remaining water to make a smooth paste. Add this to the hot soup and bring to a boil, stirring frequently. Shut off the heat and cover.

Prepare jars, lids, and pressure cooker according to manufacturer instructions.

Using a ladle and a funnel, spoon the hot soup into hot prepared jars, leaving 1 inch head space at the top of each jar.

Wipe the outer rim of the jars with a clean damp cloth to ensure a tight fit. Adjust the two-piece lids and secure snugly.

Place jars in prepared pressure cooker and process at 10 pounds pressure, or at 240°F (for pint jars this will take 75 minutes and for quart jars it will take 90 minutes).

SALADS

lthough the term "salad" often conjures up images of a few leaves of lettuce topped with slices of tomato and cucumber, salads can come in a multitude of forms and flavors. A wide variety of fresh fruit, meat, vegetables, beans, pasta, dairy, and other natural ingredients can be tossed into salads. Some salads are loaded with savory or spicy flavors. Others are delightfully sweet. Some are served chilled, while other salads taste best when still warm.

Most salads are quick and easy to prepare. They work as excellent companions for most any meal, whether it is an impromptu picnic lunch, an everyday family dinner, or an elaborate four-course meal. Many also require only a few key ingredients, most of which can be found in your own garden or your local farmers market. Salads can be made in advance and taken with you to provide a nutritious lunch when you're on the go. On hot days, a nutrient-packed salad can even provide a light, yet satisfying, meal without generating the additional heat caused by oven use.

Since the ingredients contained in salads have few limits, they are easily one of the most versatile types of food. Salads with leafy greens and lettuces along with fresh vegetable wedges can serve as an excellent complement to a variety of meat, seafood, and vegetarian dishes. Some fruit-based salads, like the naturally sweetened Tropical Fruit Salad with Guava Sauce (page 57), can even double as a dessert or tasty alternative for breakfast or brunch. Still other salads, like Asian Apple-Chicken Salad (page 44) or Moroccan Lentil and Tomato Salad (page 49), contain meat or beans that add an extra punch of protein and are able to stand alone as lunch or lighter dinners.

Asian Apple-Chicken Salad

Ingredients:

2 cups cooked chicken breast, cubed
2 cups apples, cored and cubed
2 tablespoons apple, orange, or carrot juice
2 tablespoons lime juice
1 tablespoon sesame oil
1 tablespoon mirin (rice wine)
1 tablespoon low-sodium soy sauce

1 tablespoon fresh ginger, finely grated
¼ cup fresh parsley, chopped
¼ cup fresh cilantro, chopped
3 scallions, thinly sliced
1 pound baby spinach
Pepper, to taste (optional)

Directions:

Place the chicken and apples in a large bowl. Mix the apple juice, lime juice, sesame oil, mirin, soy sauce, and ginger together in a small bowl; pour mixture over the chicken and apples. Sprinkle the parsley, cilantro, and scallions over the top and gently toss to mix. (Cover and refrigerate up to several hours, if desired.) To serve, layer the spinach on a platter and spoon the chicken mixture on top.

Dilled Granny Apple Chicken Salad

Ingredients:

2 boneless, skinless chicken breast, halved
2 Granny Smith apples, cored and chopped
2 stalks celery, sliced
1 cup halved seedless green grapes
½ cup low-fat mayonnaise
2 tablespoons chopped fresh dill
1 tablespoon fresh lemon juice

½ cup pistachio nuts, shelled
¼ teaspoon salt
Freshly ground black pepper
Boston lettuce leaves

Directions:

Place chicken breasts on a microwave-safe plate and cover with wax paper. Microwave on high for 5 minutes, rotating chicken halfway through cooking, or until chicken is cooked through. When cool enough to handle, cut chicken into bite-size chunks. In large bowl, combine chicken, apples, celery, grapes, mayonnaise, dill, lemon juice, nuts, salt, and pepper to taste until well mixed.

Serving Suggestion: Arrange lettuce leaves on platter, top with apple-chicken salad.

Curly Endive with Bacon and Pumpkin

Serves 4

Ingredients:

1 small shallot, minced
2 tablespoons cider vinegar
4 tablespoons olive oil
2 tablespoons freshly minced salad herbs
2 teaspoons grapeseed oil
¾ pound pumpkin meat, diced

6 ounces thick bacon slices, sliced into
¼-inch cut
12 cooked Brussels sprouts
8 ounces curly endive, washed and patted
dry
Salt and pepper, to taste

Directions:

In a bowl, mix the shallot, vinegar, olive oil, and herbs. Season to taste with salt and pepper. Heat the grapeseed oil and quickly sauté the diced pumpkin in a pan over medium heat. Reduce heat and continue to cook for 10-15 minutes or until tender, mixing occasionally. In another pan, sauté the bacon until barely golden brown. Add the cooked Brussels sprouts and continue to cook for 2 minutes. Mix a little bacon fat with the pumpkin at the end of the cooking time and also with the prepared dressing. Drain the bacon strips and Brussels sprouts from the remaining rendered fat. Mix the curly endive with the dressing and equally divide among four plates. Top with the warm bacon, Brussels sprouts, and diced pumpkin. Serve immediately.

Cold Pasta Salad with Char-Grilled Tomato Sauce

Courtesy of the British Tomato Growers' Association
(www.britishtomatoes.co.uk)
Serves 4

Ingredients:

2 pounds tomatoes, halved
2 red peppers, halved and de-seeded
2 teaspoons olive oil or cooking spray
Bunch of fresh basil, chopped

6 ounces farfalle tonde pasta
Salt and freshly ground pepper, to taste

Directions:

Pre-heat a grill. Put the halved tomatoes cut-side facing upwards and grill until charred. Remove from grill and cool. Put peppers on the grill, skin-side facing upwards, and brush with oil. Grill until charred, turn over peppers, and grill the other side until charred and the peppers are soft. Cool peppers in a plastic bag. Scrape the cooled tomatoes from their skins and put into a bowl. Skin the cooled peppers and cut into small pieces. Mix with the tomatoes. Stir in the chopped basil and season to taste. Cook pasta according to package instructions, making sure it is 'al dente'. Strain pasta and plunge into cold water to cool. When cool, drain thoroughly. Mix pasta with prepared tomato and pepper sauce. Serve with a baby spinach salad.

Tropical® Cheese Asian Noodle Salad

Courtesy of Tropical Cheese Industries

(www.tropicalcheese.com)

Ingredients:

1 (12 oz.) package Tropical® queso de freir
Soy sauce
Linguine
Fresh cilantro
Fresh mint
Fresh basil
Carrots
Daikon radish
Red bell pepper
Scallions

Fresh ginger
Minced garlic
Serrano chili
Chili flakes
Sesame seeds
Sesame oil
Reduced-fat peanut butter
Tamarind paste
Unrefined cane sugar
Roasted peanuts

Directions:

Combine all of the ingredients to your liking for a delicious noodle salad!

Note: The amounts for each ingredient in this recipe can be adjusted according to your own preferences.

Gingered Sweet Potato-Apple Salad

Ingredients:

15 ounces sweet potatoes or yams, cubed
8 ounces pineapple tidbits, drained
1 apple, cored and diced
½ cup diced celery
½ cup coarsely chopped cashews

¼ cup honey mustard dressing
2 teaspoons freshly grated ginger
6 cups mixed salad greens

Directions:

Combine sweet potatoes, pineapple, apple, celery and cashews in a large bowl. In a small bowl, combine honey mustard salad dressing and ginger; pour over sweet potato mixture; toss lightly. Cover and chill for at least 1 hour. Serve over salad greens.

Potato Vegetable Salad with Yogurt

Serves 6

Ingredients:

2 pounds red potatoes
2 cups broccoli florets
2 cups cauliflower florets
2 medium carrots, peeled
1 medium cucumber
¾ cup sliced radishes
½ cup sliced scallions

1 cup plain low-fat yogurt
3 tablespoons Dijon mustard
½ teaspoon salt
½ teaspoon freshly ground pepper

Directions:

Steam potatoes until they are tender. While potatoes are cooling, steam broccoli and cauliflower until slightly cooked, about 4 minutes. Set broccoli and cauliflower aside to cool. Cut carrots into thin slivers. Slice cucumber. Cut potatoes into chunks. Gently stir all vegetables together in a large mixing bowl. In another bowl, whisk together yogurt, mustard, salt and pepper. Pour yogurt dressing over vegetables and stir carefully until coated evenly. Refrigerate 1 hour before serving.

Greek Potato Salad with Feta Cheese

Courtesy of Mt. Vikos®
(www.mtvikos.com)
Serves 6

Ingredients:

2½ pounds small Red Bliss potatoes, boiled and cut in half
6-7 ounces Mt. Vikos® feta cheese, crumbled
⅓ cup pitted Kalamata olives
1 bunch scallions, chopped
⅓ cup red pepper, diced
⅓ cup extra-virgin olive oil

2 tablespoons fresh lemon juice
3 tablespoons flat-leaf parsley, finely chopped
1 teaspoon Greek oregano, dried
1 teaspoon black pepper, freshly ground
Salt, to taste

Directions:

In a salad bowl, combine cooked potatoes, Mt. Vikos® feta cheese, olives, scallions, and red pepper. In a separate bowl, whisk together remaining ingredients. Toss dressing with salad. Serve at room temperature or while potatoes are still warm.

Ginger-Carrot Salad with Cranberries

Courtesy of the American Institute for Cancer Research

(www.aicr.org)

Ingredients:

1 tablespoon freshly squeezed lemon juice

½ teaspoon honey

1 teaspoon freshly grated or finely minced ginger

⅛ teaspoon cinnamon

2 cups grated or julienned carrots (can use part cabbage)

¼ cup dried cranberries

2 tablespoons sliced almonds or peanuts

Pinch salt

Directions:

In medium bowl, whisk together lemon juice, honey, ginger, cinnamon, and salt. Toss with carrots (and cabbage, if using) and cranberries. Garnish with sliced almonds or peanuts and serve.

Garlic and Herb Lima Bean Salad

Serves 5

Ingredients:

Garlic Herb Dressing

3 tablespoons olive oil

2 tablespoons chopped green onion

3 tablespoons red wine vinegar

3 cloves garlic, minced or pressed

1 tablespoon fresh minced tarragon or 1 teaspoon dried

½ teaspoon honey

½ teaspoon salt

⅛ teaspoon ground nutmeg

Salad

5 cups cooked baby lima beans (1¾ cups dry makes about 5 cups cooked)

⅓ cup finely chopped parsley

Directions:

Garlic Herb Dressing

In a small bowl or shaker jar, combine all ingredients and mix well. Set aside.

Salad

In a large bowl combine beans, parsley, and Garlic Herb Dressing; mix well. Let stand at room temperature one hour before serving or refrigerate up to 6 hours and bring to room temperature before serving. Refrigerate leftovers.

Moroccan Lentil and Tomato Salad

Ingredients:

1¼ cups uncooked lentils
2½ cups water
3 tablespoons lemon juice
1½ tablespoons olive oil
½ teaspoon thyme
½ teaspoon mint flakes
¼ teaspoon salt

⅛ teaspoon black pepper
1 garlic clove
1½ cups quartered cherry tomatoes
1 cup diced cucumber
1½ cups crumbled reduced-fat feta cheese
1 cup thinly sliced celery
4 cups romaine lettuce leaves

Directions:

Place lentils and water in a large saucepan; bring to a boil. Cover, reduce heat, and simmer for 20 minutes or until tender. Drain well and set aside. Combine lemon juice, olive oil, thyme, mint, salt, pepper, and garlic in a medium bowl; stir with a wire whisk until blended. Add lentils, tomatoes, cucumber, cheese, and celery to dressing mixture; toss gently to coat. Serve on plates lined with romaine lettuce.

Beets and Pumpkin Salad

Serves 4

Ingredients:

6 ounces baby spinach, washed and patted dry
1 small red onion, chopped
2 red beets
¾ pound pumpkin meat, diced
¼ teaspoon Dijon mustard
4 tablespoons olive oil

2 tablespoons cider vinegar
½ teaspoon garlic clove, minced
2 tablespoons freshly minced herbed salads
2 tablespoons pumpkin seeds
Olive oil
Salt and pepper, to taste

Directions:

Preheat the oven to 375°F. Mix the mustard, oil, cider vinegar, garlic, and herbs in a large serving bowl. Season to taste and top with the baby spinach. Add the chopped onion and set aside without mixing. Place the diced pumpkin on a cookie sheet. Sprinkle olive oil and season to taste. Bake for 40 minutes or until tender. Place the beets in a saucepan and cover with water. Bring to a boil over high heat. Reduce heat and simmer for 40 minutes or until tender. Strain and let cool a bit. Peel the beets, cut in half, and slice them. Once the pumpkin is cooked, add the beets to the salad and mix with the dressing. Divide among four plates. Top each plate with the baked pumpkin, sprinkle the seeds, and serve immediately.

Note: You may serve this salad with cooked turkey or chicken slices.

Quinoa and Pumpkin Seeds Salad

Serves 4

Ingredients:

¼ cup freshly squeezed orange juice
¼ cup olive oil
2 tablespoons minced fresh ginger, divided
1 teaspoon ground cumin, divided
1 teaspoon ground cardamom, divided
1 cup quinoa
2 teaspoons olive oil
1 small yellow onion, diced
1 large garlic clove, minced

2 large carrots, diced
¾ pound diced pumpkin meat
2 cups water
¼ cup sultana raisins
¼ cup toasted pumpkin seeds
Salt and cayenne pepper, to taste
Boston lettuce leaves (enough to cover serving platter)
Freshly minced parsley, for garnish

Directions:

In a bowl, mix the orange juice, ¼ cup of olive oil, 1 tablespoon ginger, ½ teaspoon ground cumin, and ½ teaspoon ground cardamom, then season to taste. Set aside for later use. Place a coffee filter into a fine mesh sieve. Rinse the quinoa under cold water through the filter. Heat 2 teaspoons of olive oil in a saucepan over medium heat. Add the onion, garlic, carrots, and pumpkin, then quickly sauté. Add 2 cups of water, quinoa, remaining ginger, and remaining spices, then bring to a boil. Reduce heat and simmer for 20 minutes or until the liquid is completely evaporated. Mix the cooked quinoa with the dressing and refrigerate for an hour. Spread the quinoa over the prepared serving platter. Top with the raisins and pumpkin seeds. Sprinkle parsley and serve immediately.

Tomato and Asparagus Salad

Courtesy of the British Tomato Growers' Association
(www.britishtomatoes.co.uk)

Serves 4

Ingredients:

4 ounces asparagus tips
8 ounces vine ripened tomatoes, thickly sliced
1 ounce pine kernels, toasted

2 tablespoons hot horseradish sauce
4 tablespoons garlic wine vinegar
8 tablespoons extra-virgin olive oil
Crisp salad leaves

Directions:

Cook the asparagus in water for 4 to 5 minutes. Drain, rinse under cold water, and then drain again. Place asparagus, tomatoes, and pine kernels in a bowl. Whisk remaining ingredients together, then pour over tomatoes and toss together. Arrange salad leaves on plates, then spoon on tomato and asparagus.

Marinated Goat Cheese and Tomato Salad

Courtesy of the Florida Tomato Committee

(www.floridatomatoes.org)

Serves 4

Ingredients:

½ cup olive oil

½ teaspoon crushed fennel seed (see note)

½ teaspoon dried basil or several fresh basil leaves, torn into piece

1 ¼ pound (4 oz.) log goat cheese

1 head Boston lettuce, separated into leaves

2 large tomatoes, cut into wedges

3 tablespoons fresh lemon juice

1 ½ tablespoons honey

¼ cup toasted chopped pecans or walnuts (optional)

Salt and freshly ground pepper, to taste

Directions:

Blend the oil, fennel seed, basil, and pepper in a pottery bowl or pie plate. Slice the goat cheese into eight rounds and lay them in the oil. Cover and marinate at room temperature for 2 to 3 hours. When you are ready to serve the salad, arrange the salad greens on individual serving plates. Place several tomato wedges and two rounds of goat cheese on each plate, reserving the marinade. Sprinkle with toasted pecans or walnuts. Heat the lemon juice and honey in a small skillet just long enough to liquefy the honey. Whisk the lemon and honey and a pinch or two of salt into the reserved marinade and serve some of this dressing over each salad.

Note: Marinating goat cheese in olive oil, basil, and crushed fennel seeds softens the flavor of the cheese and makes it taste especially wonderful with the tomatoes. The marinade is mixed with lemon juice and honey, then used as a vinaigrette dressing with the salad. A few toasted nuts scattered on top of each salad are a nice touch.

To crush whole fennel seed, use a rolling pin.

RIPENING AND STORING TOMATOES

For the best results, store your tomatoes at room temperature and out of direct sunlight. Depending on how ripe the tomatoes are when you purchase them, they can last about a week in this state.

Your tomatoes will not ripen properly in the refrigerator, but if you don't want them to get overripe, you may store them in the refrigerator. They will last about two days in this state, but they will lose their flavor and firmness. Remove from the refrigerator 30 minutes before use to get the maximum flavor and texture.

Tomato-Avocado Salad
with Mango-Citrus Vinaigrette

Courtesy of the Ciruli Brothers

(www.champagnemango.com)

Serves 4

Ingredients:

Mango-Citrus Vinaigrette

1 orange (juice and zest)

2 Champagne® mangos, peeled and seeded

¼ cup red wine vinegar

1 teaspoon honey

1 teaspoon soy sauce

¼ teaspoon Dijon mustard

½ cup canola oil

Salt and freshly ground pepper, to taste

Salad

1 (10 oz.) package mixed greens or spring mix

1 medium avocado, peeled and sliced

2 large Roma tomatoes, cut into wedges

Directions:

Mango-Citrus Vinaigrette

In a blender, puree all vinaigrette ingredients (except the oil) on the lowest setting. Slowly drizzle in the oil until it is completely incorporated. Salt and pepper to taste.

Salad

Combine greens, avocado, and tomato in a salad bowl, then mix well. Serve salad on a plate and add just enough of the vinaigrette to coat the greens.

TOMATOES: TREAT YOUR HEART

Tomatoes are especially great for your heart! The intake of fresh tomatoes and tomato extracts has been shown to lower total cholesterol, LDL (bad) cholesterol, and triglyceride levels. Phytonutrients in tomatoes (including carotenoids, flavinoids, hydroxycinnamic acids, glycosides, and fatty acid derivatives) prevent the aggregation, or clumping, of blood platelets. This is especially helpful in preventing atherosclerosis, which is the thickening of artery walls from a buildup of fats.

Artichoke and Roasted Red Pepper Salad with Red Pepper Dressing

Serves 8

Ingredients:

Salad

8 medium artichokes, prepared and cooked as directed for whole artichokes
3 red bell peppers
Lettuce leaves
½ cup sliced red onion
½ cup sliced black olives

Dressing

1 bell pepper (roasted), reserved from salad preparation
⅓ cup balsamic vinegar
¼ cup white wine or cider vinegar
2 cloves garlic, minced
1 tablespoon chopped fresh basil or
1 teaspoon crushed dried basil
1 teaspoon chopped fresh rosemary or
½ teaspoon crushed dried rosemary

Directions:

Salad

Halve artichokes lengthwise; scoop out center petals and fuzzy centers. Remove outer leaves and reserve to garnish salad, or to use for snacks another time. Trim out hearts and slice thinly. Cover and set aside. Place whole bell peppers under pre-heated broiler; broil under high heat until charred on all sides, turning frequently with tongs. Remove from oven; place in a paper bag for 15 minutes to steam skins. Trim off stems of peppers; remove seeds and ribs. Strip off skins; slice peppers into julienne strips. Reserve ¼ of the bell pepper strips to prepare dressing. To assemble salads, arrange lettuce leaves on 8 salad plates. Arrange sliced artichoke hearts, remaining bell pepper strips, red onion and olive slices on lettuce. Garnish with a couple of cooked artichoke leaves, if desired.

Dressing

In blender or food processor container, place reserved bell pepper strips, vinegars, garlic, basil, rosemary, and sugar. Cover and process until well blended and nearly smooth. Spoon dressing over salads.

Apple, Date and Orange Salad

Ingredients:

1 cup diced apples
¾ cup dates, seeded
2 oranges

Lettuce
Salad dressing

Directions:

Peel the apples and dice them into fine pieces. Wash the dates, remove the seeds, and cut each date into six or eight pieces. Prepare the oranges as directed for preparing oranges for salad, and cut each section into two or three pieces. Just before serving, mix the fruits carefully so as not to make the salad look mushy, pile in a neat heap on garnished salad plates, and serve with any desired dressing.

Rainbow Fruit Salad

Courtesy of NHLBI, part of NIH and HHS

Ingredients:

1 large mango, peeled and diced
2 cups fresh blueberries
2 nectarines, unpeeled and sliced
2 cups halved fresh strawberries
2 cups seedless grapes
2 bananas, sliced
1 kiwifruit, peeled and diced

⅓ cup fresh orange juice
2 tablespoons lemon juice
1½ tablespoons honey
¼ teaspoon ground ginger
Dash nutmeg

Directions:

Prepare the fruit and place in a large bowl. Combine orange juice, lemon juice, honey, ginger, and nutmeg in a small bowl. Whisk together until well combined. Just before serving, pour honey orange sauce over the fruit.

Maple Fruit Salad

Courtesy of the New York State Maple Producers Association

(www.nysmaple.com)

Ingredients:

⅓ cup heavy whipping cream
½ cup pure maple syrup
⅔ cup low-fat vanilla yogurt
4 cups strawberries, sliced
2 cups pineapple chunks

1½ cups blueberries
1 cup cantaloupe chunks
¼ cup pine nuts (optional)
Pinch cinnamon

Directions:

Whisk cream until thickened, then whisk in maple syrup until mixed. Add yogurt and cinnamon. Pour over mixed fruit and add pine nuts if desired.

Fruit and Pumpkin Salad

Serves 4

Ingredients:

2 apples
1 lemon, juiced
¼ teaspoon Dijon mustard
4 tablespoons olive oil
2 tablespoons cider vinegar
½ teaspoon garlic clove, minced
2 tablespoons freshly minced basil

1 tablespoon freshly minced mint
1 small red onion, chopped
1 small cucumber, cut lengthwise and sliced
2 oranges, peeled and segmented
¾ pound pumpkin meat, medium diced
2 tablespoons chopped pecans
Salt and pepper, to taste

Directions:

Peel, core, and slice the apples. Transfer to a bowl, mix with the lemon juice, and set aside. Mix the mustard, oil, cider vinegar, garlic clove, basil, and mint in a large serving bowl. Season to taste before topping with the chopped red onion, sliced cucumber, segmented oranges, and drained apples. Set aside without mixing. Place the pumpkin in a saucepan, cover with water, and add a few pinches of salt. Bring to boil over high heat. Reduce heat and continue to simmer until tender, about 10 to 15 minutes. Strain and cool slightly before use. Mix the prepared salad with the dressing and divide among four plates. Top with the warm pumpkin and chopped pecans, and serve immediately.

Note: You may serve this salad with broiled or baked salmon.

Summer Greens Salad with Sweetened Dried Cranberries and Cranberry Vinaigrette

Courtesy of Cape Cod Cranberry Growers' Association, Carver, MA

(www.cranberries.org)

Serves 4

Ingredients:

Vinaigrette

¼ cup extra-virgin olive oil

2 tablespoons cranberry juice cocktail

1 tablespoon apple cider vinegar

1 tablespoon balsamic vinegar

2 teaspoons minced shallots

Salt and pepper, to taste

Salad

¼ cup walnut pieces, lightly toasted

2 cups mesclun greens, washed

1 head Belgian endive, yellow tipped, cored, and cut lengthwise into narrow strips

½ cup red onion, sliced in lengths

1 bunch watercress, washed

¼ cup sweetened dried cranberries

Directions:

Vinaigrette

In small bowl whisk together the olive oil, cranberry juice cocktail, vinegars, and shallots. Season with salt and pepper to taste. Let stand for at least ½ hour to allow flavors to blend.

Salad

In small dry frying pan, over medium heat, toast the walnuts, shaking the pan often, until brown and aromatic. Transfer to small bowl and set aside. Divide the mesclun greens among four individual salad plates. Top with cut endive, onion, and watercress. Add toasted walnut pieces and sweetened dried cranberries. Top with 2 tablespoons of vinaigrette.

"If you tickle the earth with a hoe she laughs with a harvest."
—Douglas William Jerrold

Tropical Fruit Salad with Guava Sauce

Ingredients:

2 bananas, sliced
1 ripe pear, sliced
4 kiwis, peeled and sliced
2 cups sliced strawberries

2 feijoas, sliced (optional)
2 tablespoons orange juice concentrate
1 ripe guava

Directions:

Combine all of the ingredients, except for the juice and guava, in a large serving bowl. Peel and slice the guava into quarters and place in a blender with the orange juice concentrate. Puree until smooth. Pour the mixture through a sieve to remove the seeds and pour over the fruit salad.

STRAWBERRIES: A DELICIOUS SHELL

The small, yellow seed-like pieces (called achenes) on the surface of a strawberry are the real fruit of the plant. The red pulp of the berry is actually the shell.

FISH & SEAFOOD ENTRÉES

A peaceful feeling settles over you as you sit on the dock with the sun slowly rising above the surrounding mountains. You let your bare feet graze the surface of the water as you are lulled by the gentle bobbing of your fishing line as it keeps rhythm with the sway of the water before you. A sudden tug on the line breaks the tempo and you spring into action to reel in the first catch of the day. If your success continues, you and your family will feast on fresh fish tonight.

While you may enjoy the appeal of sitting lakeside and catching your fish one at a time, if you are fortunate to have a local seafood market, you might also choose to support your local fishing industry and purchase fresh fish, lobsters, crab, and shellfish and prepare an entrée like Honey Glazed Salmon (page 62) served on a bed of rice or a fun and tasty meal of Simple Fish Tacos (page 60).

Regardless of the route you choose to obtain your seafood items, one fact is undeniable. The flavor and health benefits of entrées prepared with fresh seafood and fish, especially when paired with fresh and organic vegetables, are unparalleled to their frozen or processed counterparts.

Simple Fish Tacos

Serves 6

Ingredients:

½ cup fat-free sour cream
¼ cup fat-free mayonnaise
½ cup chopped fresh cilantro
½ package low-sodium taco seasoning, divided
4 cod or white fish fillets (1 pound total), cut into 1-inch pieces

1 tablespoon olive oil
2 tablespoons lemon juice
12 (6-inch) corn tortillas, warmed
2 cups shredded red and green cabbage
2 cups diced tomato
Lime wedges, for serving
Taco sauce, for serving

Directions:

In a small bowl, combine sour cream, mayonnaise, cilantro, and 2 tablespoons seasoning mix. In medium bowl, combine cod, olive oil, lemon juice, and remaining seasoning mix; pour into large skillet. Cook, stirring constantly, over medium-high heat for 4 to 5 minutes or until cod flakes easily when tested with a fork. Fill warm tortillas with fish mixture. Top with cabbage, tomato, sour cream mixture, lime wedges, and taco sauce.

Ginger-Cran Leek Glazed Salmon

Courtesy of Cape Cod Cranberry Growers' Association, Carver, MA
(www.cranberries.org)

Ingredients:

2 cups whole cranberries
½ cup brown sugar
1 tablespoon fresh ginger (or ½ teaspoon dried)
1 leek, clean well and cut in rings
1 tablespoon olive oil
1 pound salmon

Directions:

Gently cook cranberries, sugar, and ginger until cranberries are soft (5–10 minutes). Sauté leek in oil. Combine leek and cranberries, then ladle over salmon. Broil salmon to your liking (best if cooked medium rare). Can be served with rice.

Fish and Tomato Thai Curry

Courtesy of the British Tomato Growers' Association
(www.britishtomatoes.co.uk)
Serves 6

Ingredients:

Curry Sauce

3 shallots, finely chopped
2 cloves garlic, finely chopped
2 bird's eye chilies, seeds removed and
finely chopped
3 kaffir lime leaves
2 inches galangal (or ginger), scraped and
cut into 4 pieces
2 sticks lemongrass, trimmed and cut
lengthways
1 bunch coriander, chopped
1 teaspoon green Thai curry paste
1¼ teaspoons shrimp paste
1 cup reduced-fat coconut milk
1 cup semi-skimmed milk

Fish

1 pound, 2 ounces plum tomatoes
1½ pounds firm white fish (such as
monkfish or Antarctic icefish)
1¼ cups Thai fragrant rice

Directions:

Curry Sauce

Prepare the ingredients for the curry sauce. Put them all into a saucepan and bring slowly to a boil, stirring constantly. Cover and simmer for 5 minutes. Cool, then remove lime leaves, galangal (or ginger), and lemongrass with a slotted spoon and discard. Pour sauce into a blender and pulse until smooth.

Fish

Skin and quarter the tomatoes. Cut fish into 1-inch cubes. Cook rice according to package instructions. Put tomatoes and fish into a large saucepan. Pour the sauce over the fish and tomatoes. Bring slowly to a boil and simmer for 6 minutes or until fish is cooked. Serve on rice.

Note: Try finding Thai curry packs in the fresh produce section of your supermarket—they contain most of the ingredients required for the sauce.

Honey Glazed Salmon

Courtesy of Janette Marshall from Health Benefits of Honey
(www.health-benefits-of-honey.com)

Ingredients:

1 fresh salmon fillet per person
2 cloves garlic, crushed
4-6 scallions, chopped
2 tablespoons honey
¼ cup oil

⅛ cup balsamic vinegar
⅛ cup soy sauce
Small dash sesame oil
¼ teaspoon sea salt
1 tablespoon raw brown sugar

Directions:

Blend together all ingredients (except the salmon) to create a marinade. Place the fish fillets into a large, flat oven-proof glass dish. Make sure to oil the dish first to prevent the salmon from sticking while cooking. Pour the marinade over the fillets, cover with plastic wrap, and leave in the refrigerator overnight. This allows the fish to absorb all those wonderful flavors. Set oven to medium heat. Remove marinated fish from the refrigerator and remove the plastic wrap from the dish. Tip the dish slightly and spoon the marinade over the salmon so that it is equally covered. Place in the oven for approximately 20 minutes. Check to see if the salmon is cooked by pulling at the flesh with a fork. It is cooked once it appears to be flaking. Remove from the oven and set aside. In a saucepan, slowly heat (not boil) a little more balsamic vinegar and another spoonful of honey. Place the cooked fish onto pre-heated plates or a serving dish and pour the excess marinade into the saucepan. Stir this extra sauce together and pour over salmon. Decorate with a few herb leaves and thin slices of either lemon, lime, or orange or a rich tomato salsa.

Honey-Mustard Salmon

Ingredients:

4 tablespoons honey
3 tablespoons mustard (Dijon works well)
2 teaspoons lemon juice
4 (6 oz.) salmon steaks
Pepper, to taste

Directions:

Preheat oven to 350°F. Mix the honey, mustard, and lemon juice in a small dish. Coat the salmon steaks with the mixture. Season with pepper. Wrap the salmon steaks and the extra sauce in foil and place them in a medium baking dish. Bake for approximately 25 to 30 minutes, or until the fish flakes easily when poked with a fork. Drizzle a little of the remaining sauce over the salmon steaks and serve hot with a side of rice.

Maple Mustard Salmon

Courtesy of the Massachusetts Maple Producers Association

(www.massmaple.org)

Ingredients:

4 salmon fillets
⅔ cup melted butter
½ tablespoon dried dill
½ cup pure maple syrup
¼ cup Dijon mustard

Directions:

Blend all ingredients (except salmon) over low heat until melted together. Grill or broil salmon, basting and turning until flaky and fully cooked.

Shrimp, Tomatoes, and Barrel-Aged Feta Cheese

Courtesy of Mt. Vikos®

(www.mtvikos.com)

Ingredients:

10 ounces medium-sized shrimp, peeled and deveined
6 ounces Mt. Vikos® barrel-aged feta cheese, crumbled
2 fresh tomatoes, medium, cut into large chunks
¼ cup pitted Kalamata olives
3 tablespoons extra-virgin olive oil
3 tablespoons fresh, flat-leaf parsley, finely chopped
2 cloves fresh garlic, chopped
1 teaspoon oregano, dried
½ teaspoon salt
½ teaspoon black pepper, freshly ground

Directions:

Preheat oven to 350°F. Mix all the ingredients and place in a small baking casserole. Bake, uncovered, for 30-35 minutes. Serve immediately. Serves four as an appetizer or six as a main dish with pasta.

Shrimp Pasta in Garlic and Basil Cream Sauce

Courtesy of Cornerstone Garlic Farm

Ingredients:

12 ounces penne or other pasta
1 pound medium shrimp, peeled
10 cloves spicy hardneck garlic, divided
4 tablespoons butter, divided
1 medium shallot, minced

1 cup heavy cream
10-12 basil leaves, minced
1½ cups freshly grated Parmesan, divided
Salt and pepper, to taste

Directions:

Cook pasta as directed on the box. In a small, deep skillet sauté the shrimp and two cloves of garlic (pressed) in 1 tablespoon of butter until done. Take shrimp out of the pan and add the rest of the butter. Add six more cloves of garlic (pressed) and shallots. Sauté for 3 minutes over low heat. Pour in cream, basil, 1 cup cheese, two cloves of garlic (thinly sliced), salt, and pepper. Simmer over low heat, covered but vented, until thickened, 7-10 minutes. Add the shrimp back in the pan, mix with sauce, pour over pasta, and top with remaining cheese and a basil leaf.

Simple Shrimp and Garlic Sauté

Courtesy of Nina MacDonald, Toronto Garlic Festival

(www.torontogarlicfestival.ca)

Ingredients:

6 medium-sized shrimp
¼ cup canola oil
4 cloves garlic, minced
1 teaspoon kosher salt
Freshly ground black pepper, to taste
1 tablespoon clarified butter

Directions:

Combine shrimp, oil, garlic, salt, and pepper in a bowl. Gently stir to combine ingredients. Cover and set in the refrigerator overnight. Heat a non-stick or seasoned skillet to low or medium heat. Add butter. When a few drops of water dance in the pan, add the shrimp. Cook until pinkish red. Additional garlic may be added one minute before serving (don't let the garlic burn). Serve with lemon wedge.

Note: This recipe makes two side dish servings. By using more shrimp, it can be served as a main course. Prawns or shrimp can be used.

Honey Walnut Shrimp

Courtesy of Janette Marshall from Health Benefits of Honey
(www.health-benefits-of-honey.com)

Ingredients:

1 tablespoon butter
1 cup whole shelled walnuts
3 tablespoons sugar
3 tablespoons mayonnaise
1 tablespoon honey
2 tablespoons sweetened condensed milk
½ teaspoon lemon juice

1 cup flour
½ teaspoon salt
1 cup water
2-3 cups good-quality cooking oil, for the wok
1 pound shrimp, shelled and cleaned

Directions:

Heat the butter in a pan over medium heat until melted. Add the walnuts and stir constantly for one minute. Add 2 tablespoons sugar and continue stirring all these ingredients together for 2 minutes.

Sauce

Mix together the mayonnaise, honey, sweetened condensed milk, and lemon juice. Set the sauce aside.

Shrimp Batter

Mix together the flour, remaining teaspoon of sugar, salt, and water. Stir these ingredients until smooth.

Shrimp

Heat 2 to 3 cups of cooking oil in a wok. Add shrimp to the batter and, using a fork to pick them out, shake any excess batter off and place into the hot oil. (It is recommended to use 8 to 10 shrimp at a time to avoid overloading the wok.) Cook the shrimp until they become a light golden brown color. Repeat and when each batch is ready, place them on paper towels to soak up the excess oil. Once the shrimp are all cooked, stir them into your sauce and serve.

Pasta with Tomatoes, Shrimp, and Feta

Courtesy of the Florida Tomato Committee

(www.floridatomatoes.org)

Serves 4-6

Ingredients:

1 cup olive oil

4 green onions, finely chopped

1 green bell pepper, seeded and finely chopped

1 teaspoon hot pepper flakes

1 tablespoon fresh (or 1 teaspoon dried) oregano, finely chopped

½ cup Italian parsley, finely chopped

1 pound medium shrimp, peeled and deveined

4 medium firm, ripe tomatoes, peeled, seeded and chopped

1 tablespoon tomato paste

½ cup white wine

1 pound penne pasta

½ pound feta cheese, crumbled

Salt and freshly ground pepper, to taste

Directions:

Warm oil in a large skillet over medium heat. Add green onions and cook, stirring constantly, until transparent (about 5 minutes). Add bell peppers, hot pepper flakes, oregano, and parsley. Salt and pepper to taste and cook, stirring constantly, until peppers are soft. Reduce heat to medium-low. Add shrimp and cook until they are no longer pink. Add the tomatoes and cook until they release their juices. Add tomato paste and white wine and cook for about 20 minutes. Set aside and keep warm in the oven. Bring 5 quarts of water to a boil. Add pasta and 1 teaspoon salt. Stir and cook until firm to the bite, about 8 to 10 minutes. Drain the pasta and toss with the sauce. Sprinkle feta cheese over top. Serve immediately.

Note: This very sophisticated and light pasta dish is delightful with crusty bread and a light green salad for a very special summertime meal.

Bacon Wrapped Scallops with Mango Maple Glaze

Courtesy of the New York State Maple Producers Association

(www.nysmaple.com)

Ingredients:

8 scallops

4 strips bacon

½ cup pure maple syrup

1 cup mango sauce

Directions:

Preheat oven to 400°F. Wrap each scallop with ½ strip of bacon. Place in a small baking dish. Mix the maple syrup and mango sauce well. Baste and bake the scallops for 20 minutes until nearly cooked. Baste again and then place under broiler for an additional 10 minutes or until bacon begins to crisp.

Seared Scallops with Pumpkin Timbale

Serves 4

Ingredients:

2 teaspoons olive oil
2 teaspoons butter
1 pound dry sea scallops
Salt and pepper, to taste
Pumpkin timbale (see page 99)

Directions:

Rinse and pat dry the scallops. Lightly season the scallops with salt and pepper. Heat the oil and butter in a large saucepan over medium-high heat. Add the scallops and cook until golden brown on both sides, about 2 minutes per side. Serve immediately with the timbale.

Fresh Corn, Tomato, and Scallop Pasta

Courtesy of the National Pasta Association
(www.Ilovepasta.org)
Serves 6

Ingredients:

1 pound medium shells, ziti, or other medium pasta shape, uncooked
1 tablespoon plus 1 teaspoon olive or vegetable oil
¾ cup sliced red onion
1 pound bay scallops or medium shrimp, peeled and deveined
1 cup fresh or frozen corn kernels (2 ears)
2 cloves garlic, minced

4 large ripe tomatoes, peeled, seeded, and diced (about 4 cups)
2 tablespoons minced fresh oregano
½ teaspoon dried rosemary
½–1 teaspoon hot sauce
2 tablespoons red wine vinegar
1 tablespoon e lemon juice
½ cup crumbled feta cheese
Salt and freshly ground pepper, to taste

Directions:

Prepare pasta according to package directions. While pasta is cooking, heat 1 tablespoon oil in a large skillet. Add red onion and cook for about 2 minutes. Add scallops, corn, and garlic. Cook for 4 minutes, stirring often. Add tomatoes, oregano, rosemary, and hot sauce. Simmer just until scallops are done and mixture is thoroughly heated, about 5 minutes. Stir in red wine vinegar and lemon juice. When pasta is done, drain well. Transfer to a serving bowl. Drizzle with remaining 1 teaspoon oil and toss well. Spoon tomato mixture over pasta. Sprinkle with cheese, salt, and pepper. Serve immediately.

FISH & SEAFOOD ENTREES

Crispy Angel Hair Cakes with Scallops, Escarole, and Tomato Coulis

Courtesy of the National Pasta Association

(www.Ilovepasta.org)

Serves 4

Ingredients:

8 ounces angel hair pasta

6 plum tomatoes, quartered

5 cloves garlic, peeled and coarsely chopped

4 teaspoons olive oil, divided

8 sea scallops

4 ounces pancetta, diced

1 large shallot, minced

1 small head escarole, washed, trimmed, and chopped

4 basil sprigs, for garnishing

Salt and freshly ground black pepper, to taste

Directions:

Preheat the oven to 450°F. Cook the pasta according to package directions. Rinse, drain, and set aside. On a baking sheet with sides, toss together the tomatoes, garlic, 1 teaspoon olive oil, and salt and pepper. Roast the tomatoes until they are very soft, about 20 minutes. Remove the tomatoes and reduce the oven temperature to 375°F. While the tomatoes are roasting, make the pasta cakes. Warm 1 teaspoon olive oil in a small, non-stick sauté pan over medium-high heat. Add a generous ½ cup of pasta to the pan and flatten it into a pancake shape. Fry on both sides until golden brown. Transfer to a baking sheet. Make three more cakes in the same way and then four small, lacy cakes to use as tops. Set the cakes aside until needed. When the tomatoes are ready, puree them in a blender or food processor until smooth. Strain into a saucepan, cover, and set over very low heat until needed.

Shrimp with Pumpkin and Zucchini Fettuccini

Serves 4

Ingredients:

1 tablespoon olive oil

1 pound shrimp, peeled and deveined

6 ounces whole-wheat fettuccini

2 strips bacon, sliced

1 medium onion, diced small

1 small leek, white part only, diced small

6 ounces pumpkin meat, diced small

6 ounces green zucchini, diced small

2 garlic cloves, minced

¼ cup white wine

4 ounces cream

2 tablespoons freshly minced basil

Salt and pepper, to taste

Directions:

Cook the fettuccini according to package instructions. Place the wine in a saucepan and reduce by half. Heat the oil in a saucepan over high heat. Add the bacon and brown. Add the onion and leek, then sauté for a minute. Add the pumpkin, zucchini, garlic, and shrimp, then lightly brown. Add reduced wine, cream, and basil, then reduce to a creamy consistency. Strain the pasta and mix them with the mixture. Season to taste and serve immediately.

Mini Maple Crab Cakes

Courtesy of the New York State Maple Producers Association

(www.nysmaple.com)

Ingredients:

1 (16 oz.) can crabmeat, squeezed dry
½ cup pure maple syrup
1 tablespoon Dijon or whole grain mustard
1½ teaspoons Old Bay® seasoning
1 teaspoon cajun seasoning
½ green bell pepper, finely diced
½ red bell pepper, finely diced
1 tablespoon finely minced shallots
2 eggs
½ lime, juiced
½ lime, zested
1½ cups Panko breadcrumbs
1¼ teaspoons salt
½ teaspoon black pepper
½ teaspoons Tabasco sauce
Oil, as needed
Panko breadcrumbs, as needed

Maple Cream Sauce

½ cup sour cream
1 tablespoon pure maple cream
½ teaspoon lime juice
¼ teaspoon lime zest
¼ teaspoon Tabasco sauce
Salt and pepper, to taste

Directions:

Combine all ingredients in a large bowl. Mix well. Let mixture sit and absorb moisture for about 5 minutes. Form into mini patties. When ready to cook, heat a large sauté pan over high heat until hot. Add enough oil to slightly coat the bottom of the pan. Dredge each mini crab cake in more panko breadcrumbs. Cook each crab cake over medium to medium-high heat until golden, flip once, and cook until golden. Place crab cakes on a sheet tray and finish baking in a 450°F oven until the internal temperature reaches 165°F.

Maple Cream Sauce

Whisk together sauce ingredients in a small bowl. Let sit 10 minutes to meld flavors. Place a small dollop on top of each crab cake and serve.

Mussels with Tomato Wine Sauce

Courtesy of the Florida Tomato Committee
(www.floridatomatoes.org)
Serves 5

Ingredients:

2 pounds mussels
¼ cup water
1 tablespoon unsalted butter
1 small onion, minced
1 clove garlic, minced
4 large tomatoes, cored, seeded, and coarsely chopped
¾ cup dry white wine
1 tablespoon minced fresh parsley
Salt and freshly ground pepper, to taste

Directions:

Scrub the mussels under cold running water, pulling off the "beards" with your hands. Put the water in a large pot, add the mussels, cover, and place on a burner with the heat turned off. Melt the butter in a medium-sized saucepan. Add the onion and sauté, stirring over medium heat for 2 minutes. Stir in the garlic, sauté for 30 seconds, then add the tomatoes. Turn the burner under the mussels to high. Cook the tomatoes for 2 minutes, then add the wine and season to taste. Quickly bring the tomatoes to a boil and boil for about 5 to 8 minutes, until the sauce is as thick as you like. Stir in the parsley and keep the sauce over very low heat. Meanwhile, steam the mussels for about 6 to 8 minutes, until they've opened. Discard any that don't open. Arrange the mussels on serving plates. Spread the shells slightly, or break off the empty half, and spoon some of the sauce over each mussel. Serve immediately.

Note: Mussels over pasta or rice make an inexpensive appetizer or main course. Here they are served as a main course, so you may want to double the sauce so you have extra for the pasta.

Curried Conch, Mango, and Tomato Chowder

Courtesy of the Ciruli Brothers

(www.champagnemango.com)

Serves 4

Ingredients:

1 tablespoon olive oil

1 carrot, diced

1 stick celery, diced

1 onion, diced

1 ear corn, roasted and cut off the cob

1 pound conch meat, sliced very thin (you may substitute with shrimp)

2 slightly green Champagne® mangos, diced

2 tablespoons yellow curry paste

2 tomatoes, chopped

1 stalk lemongrass, cut into 1-inch strips and lightly crushed with the flat of a knife

1 cup chicken stock or water

1 (14 oz.) can coconut milk

1 teaspoon chopped chives

1 teaspoon chopped cilantro

Directions:

In a medium saucepan, combine oil, carrot, celery, onion, and corn. Sauté for 30 seconds, then add the conch. Sauté for an additional 30 seconds then add the diced mango and curry paste. Cook for an additional 30 seconds and then add the tomatoes, lemongrass, chicken stock, and coconut milk. Simmer for 4–5 minutes on low. Add the herbs and serve.

Tuna, Tomato, and Bean Salad

Ingredients:

Dressing

½ teaspoon grated lemon peel

⅓ cup lemon juice

¼ cup olive oil

2 tablespoon fresh chopped parsley

1 teaspoon rosemary

1 tablespoon Dijon mustard

Salad

3 medium green bell peppers

3 medium red bell peppers

2 (15 oz.) cans white beans, rinsed and drained

2 (6 oz.) cans water packed tuna, drained

½ cup sliced ripe olives

1 head lettuce

2 medium tomatoes, cut into wedges

Directions:

Dressing

Mix all dressing ingredients thoroughly in a tightly covered container.

Salad

Set oven to broil. Place the bell peppers on the broiler pan. Broil with the tops 4 to 5 inches from the heat for about 10 minutes on each side or until the skin blisters and browns. Remove from oven. Wrap in towel; let stand for 5 minutes. Remove skin, stems, seeds, and membranes of the peppers. Cut peppers into ¼-inch slices. Toss peppers, beans, tuna, olives, and dressing in a bowl. Cover and chill for 4 hours, stirring occasionally. Spoon salad onto lettuce leaves and garnish with tomato wedges.

FISH & SEAFOOD ENTREES

MEAT & POULTRY ENTRÉES

Baked, fried, broiled, grilled, roasted, diced, breaded, ground, shredded, blackened, fileted, or served on a bun… Whatever the form or cooking method, meat and poultry dishes abound in America. Beef, pork, chicken, and turkey are some of the most common ingredients featured in lunch and dinner entrées found on grills and plates in homes and restaurants all across the country.

Appreciated for their taste as well as their capability to appease voracious appetites and provide fuel for the body, beef, chicken, turkey, and pork are basic ingredients for meat eaters. Poultry and meat dishes help provide essential proteins and other important vitamins and minerals that your body requires. Of course, fattier cuts of meat and poultry often produce more flavors in foods because of the fats they contain. They can also be sources of unhealthy fats and cholesterols in your diet. When selecting meat and poultry for your dishes, it is advisable to opt for leaner cuts and to make the effort to trim away excess fat before eating them.

Recipes found in this section, like mouth-watering Broiled Sirloin with Spicy Mustard and Apple Chutney (page 84) and Chicken Chili (page 78), pair lean cuts of meat and poultry with fresh fruits and vegetables, as well as other nutritious ingredients, to produce a delicious and healthy combination.

Apple Chicken Stir-Fry

Ingredients:

1 pound cubed boneless, skinless, chicken breast
1 tablespoon vegetable oil
½ cup onion, vertically sliced
1¾ cups (3-4 medium) carrots, thinly sliced
1 teaspoon dried basil, crushed
1 cup fresh or frozen Chinese pea pods

1 tablespoon water
1 medium baking apple, cored and thinly sliced
2 cups cooked brown rice

Directions:

Stir-fry cubed chicken breast in 1 tablespoon vegetable oil in nonstick skillet until lightly browned and cooked. Remove from skillet. Stir-fry onion, carrots and basil in oil in same skillet until carrots are tender. Stir in pea pods and water; stir-fry for 2 minutes. Remove from heat; stir in apple. Add to chicken, serve hot over cooked rice.

Chicken Teriyaki Maple Stir Fry

Courtesy of the New York State Maple Producers Association
(www.nysmaple.com)

Ingredients:

4 teaspoons canola oil
1 tablespoon fresh minced garlic
1 pound boneless chicken breasts, cut into bite-sized strips
¼ cup teriyaki sauce
1 cup red pepper, cut into bite-sized strips
2 cups zucchini, cut into bite-sized strips

2 cups sliced mushrooms
1 cup snow peas
1 tablespoon soy sauce
1½ tablespoons pure maple cream
1–2 dashes hot sauce, to taste (optional)

Directions:

Heat oil in wok until hot. Add fresh minced garlic and sauté until golden (1-2 minutes). Add chicken strips. Toss while cooking. After chicken is partially cooked (about 4 minutes) add teriyaki sauce and continue to toss to blend. Cook chicken until done. Remove chicken from pan with a slotted spoon. Set aside. Add red pepper strips and toss with spoon while cooking for about 1 minute. Continue to add vegetables in order listed, letting each addition heat and cook before adding the next (about a minute or so). Sprinkle soy sauce over vegetables and add a little more teriyaki sauce if needed. When vegetables are the desired doneness, add maple cream and toss to coat hot vegetables. Return chicken to pan and toss together with the vegetables until chicken is hot. If needed, add a little additional teriyaki sauce and hot sauce, if using. Serve over rice.

Chicken Breast Stuffed with Wild Rice and Cranberry Stuffing

Courtesy of Cape Cod Cranberry Growers' Association, Carver, MA

(www.cranberries.org)

Serves 6

Ingredients:

Chicken

6 chicken breast halves, cleaned and tenders removed

Wild Rice and Cranberry Stuffing

Egg wash (3 eggs in bowl, beaten with fork)

Flour with salt and pepper added to taste

2 tablespoons olive oil

Wild Rice and Cranberry Stuffing

3 cups cooked wild rice

1 cup bread crumbs

1 cup sweetened dried cranberries

½ cup chopped walnuts

½ cup fresh chopped apples (peeled and cored)

½ cup melted butter

¼ cup orange juice

¼ cup cranberry juice cocktail

Directions:

Chicken

Heat oven to 350°F. With a sharp knife, cut a pocket down the side of the chicken breast about ¾ of the way through. Stuff with Wild Rice and Cranberry Stuffing. Heat large skillet over medium-high heat for one minute, then add 2 tablespoons of olive oil. Dip stuffed chicken breast in egg wash, and dredge through flour. Place stuffed chicken breast in hot skillet. Brown stuffed chicken breast for one minute on each side, remove from skillet, and place in shallow baking dish. Bake in 350°F oven for 30 minutes. Remove from oven and slice each breast crosswise about ½-inch thick. Place on serving platter over greens.

Wild Rice and Cranberry Stuffing

Combine all ingredients in mixing bowl and mix well. After stuffing chicken breasts, freeze remaining stuffing for future use.

CRANBERRIES: PLAY WITH YOUR FOOD

Cranberries bounce and float! The fruit has small air pockets inside that make them bounce when they are ripe. It also causes them to float on water.

Roasted Chicken with Pumpkin Risotto

Serves 4

Ingredients:

1-4 pounds roasting chicken
2 tablespoons olive oil
2 teaspoons dried thyme, minced
4 ounces onions, diced (about 1 small onion, diced)
1 tablespoon garlic cloves, minced
12 ounces Arborio rice

¼ cup Chardonnay wine
4-5 cups chicken stock (low-fat and low-sodium)
¼ cup Parmesan cheese, grated
¼ cup cream, hot
8 ounces cooked diced pumpkin meat, hot
Salt and pepper, to taste

Directions:

Preheat the oven to 325°F. Remove giblets from the chicken. Rinse the chicken and pat dry. Season the chicken cavity with salt and pepper. Brush 1 tablespoon of olive oil all over the chicken and sprinkle 1 teaspoon of thyme over it. Place the chicken in a roasting pan and roast for 2 to 2½ hours or until the juices run clear. Heat the remaining oil in a pan over high heat. Add the onions and sauté until translucent. Add the garlic and rice, then stir for 1 minute. Add the wine and remaining thyme, then cook over medium heat until the liquid is evaporated. Add half of the stock and simmer, uncovered. Once the liquid is absorbed, add the remaining stock and continue to simmer, uncovered. Once the stock is almost absorbed, check the rice. It should be cooked through before going on. If not quite done, keep adding more stock and cook until almost evaporated again. Add the Parmesan, cream, and herbs, then season to taste and bring to a simmer. Remove from heat, gently add the cooked diced pumpkin, and cover for 2 minutes before serving with the roasted chicken.

THE HISTORY OF PUMPKINS

Centuries ago, Native Americans recognized the many uses for pumpkins—a member of the Cucurbita family, which also includes squash, watermelon, and cucumbers—and included them as a staple in their diets. The early settlers and explorers later incorporated them into their eating regimen as well, and carried the seeds with them when they returned to Europe, further spreading the cultivation and popularity of pumpkins. Today, over 1.5 billion pounds of pumpkins are produced annually in the United States, making it one of the world's leading pumpkin producers. Other top world producers include Mexico, India, and China.

Roasted Chicken Legs with Jalapeño and Tomato

Courtesy of Greensgrow Farm

(www.greensgrow.org)

Serves 2

Ingredients:

1 tablespoon olive oil

2 teaspoons fresh lime juice

2 whole chicken legs (about 1 pound total)

2 small tomatoes, cut into ½-inch slices

2 jalapeño chilies, seeded (if desired) and cut into ¼-inch slices

1 small onion, cut into ¼-inch slices

1 garlic clove, sliced thin

½ cup low-sodium chicken broth

Salt and freshly ground pepper, to taste

Directions:

Preheat oven to 450°F. In a bowl, stir together the oil and lime juice. Add the chicken legs and toss to coat. Arrange the chicken legs, skin side facing upwards, in a roasting pan and season with salt and pepper. Add tomatoes, chilies, onion, garlic, and salt to the oil mixture and toss well. Spread the vegetable mixture around the chicken legs in one layer and roast for 30 minutes on the upper rack of an oven, until chicken is cooked through. Transfer chicken to a platter and keep warm, covered with foil. Add broth to the vegetables in the pan and boil over medium-high heat, scraping up browned bits until sauce thickens slightly, about 2 to 3 minutes. Serve chicken with sauce and vegetables.

Turkey-Apple Gyros

Ingredients:

1 medium Golden Delicious apple, cored and thinly sliced

2 tablespoons fresh lemon juice

1 cup thinly sliced onion

1 medium red bell pepper, cut into thin strips

1 medium green bell pepper, cut into thin strips

1 teaspoon olive oil

8 ounces cooked turkey breast, cut into thin strips

6 whole-wheat pita bread rounds, lightly toasted

½ cup plain low-fat yogurt

1 garlic clove, minced

Directions:

Toss apple with lemon juice; set aside. In a large nonstick skillet, sauté onion and peppers in hot oil, stirring frequently until crisp-tender. Add turkey to skillet and stir until heated through. Stir in apple mixture. Add garlic to yogurt and mix. Fold pitas in half and fill with turkey mixture. Drizzle with yogurt mixture.

MEAT & POULTRY ENTREES

Chicken Chili

Courtesy of Hood River Garlic Farm

(www.hoodrivergarlic.com)

Serves 8

Ingredients:

¼ cup extra-virgin olive oil

½ cup chopped onion

5 garlic cloves, pressed

1 large Anaheim pepper, chopped with seeds removed

2 jalapeño peppers, chopped with seeds removed

3 tablespoons chili powder (up to 4 tablespoons)

1 tablespoon cumin

2 (35 oz.) cans stewed tomatoes, crushed

2 tablespoons tomato paste

¾ cup chicken stock

1 bag homemade black beans (see page 119), thawed

1 teaspoon dried oregano

4 cups shredded, cooked chicken meat

Salt and pepper, to taste

Shredded cheddar cheese, cilantro and sour cream, for garnish

Directions:

In a large sauce pan, add olive oil and onions. Cook over medium-high heat, stirring frequently, until golden, about 5 minutes. Add garlic, peppers, chili powder, cumin and sauté for 3 minutes. Add more olive oil if needed. Add tomatoes, tomato paste, stock, black beans, oregano, salt, pepper, and cooked chicken meat. Bring mixture to a simmer and reduce heat to low. Simmer, uncovered, for an hour, stirring frequently. Salt and pepper to taste.

Maple Chicken

Courtesy of Shaver-Hill Farm

(www.shaverhillfarm.com)

Ingredients:

1 (2½-3 lb.) chicken

¼ cup melted butter

½ cup pure maple syrup

½ teaspoon grated lemon rind

½ teaspoon salt

¼ cup chopped almonds (optional)

2 teaspoons lemon juice

Dash pepper

Directions:

Place chicken pieces in shallow baking pan. Mix remaining ingredients and pour evenly over chicken. Bake uncovered for 1 hour at 325°F, basting occasionally.

Exotic Grilled Honey Wings

Courtesy of Benefits of Honey, the number one ranked website on the health benefits of honey (www.benefits-of-honey.com)

Ingredients:
Marinade
5 cloves garlic, crushed
5 ginger slices
1 teaspoon five spices powder
1 teaspoon black pepper
2 teaspoons salt
1 tablespoon soy sauce
1 teaspoon dark soy sauce

1 tablespoon honey (such as macadamia honey)
1 egg

Wings
8 chicken wings
8 wooden skewers
2 tablespoons honey, for glazing during grilling

Directions:
Marinade

Combine all ingredients and set aside.

Wings

Place wings onto wooden skewers for easy grilling. Marinate wings in prepared mixture for at least 5 hours. Grill wings in the oven at 435°F for 15 minutes, then glaze each of them with honey using a baking brush. Grill for 10 minutes more, turn over to the other side, and glaze with honey again before grilling for the final 10 minutes. Serve while hot.

Honey Bourbon Chicken

Courtesy of Janette Marshall from Health Benefits of Honey
(www.health-benefits-of-honey.com)

Ingredients:
4 boneless chicken breasts
1 cup flour
2 red onions, chopped
2 cloves garlic
2 stalks celery
½ pint chicken stock
2 teaspoons mustard

2 teaspoons Worcestershire sauce
1 tablespoon honey
1 tablespoon bourbon
Salt and pepper, to taste

Directions:

Dice and flour the washed and dried chicken pieces. Set them aside. Chop the red onions, garlic cloves, and celery. Fry these gently together until soft. In a large pan, add chicken stock, mustard, Worcestershire sauce, honey, and bourbon. Salt and pepper to taste. Stir all ingredients together, add the chicken pieces, and place in a casserole dish. Cook in the center of a 400°F oven for approximately an hour.

Garlic Burgers

Courtesy of Hood River Garlic Farm

(www.hoodrivergarlic.com)

Serves 4

Ingredients:

5 or 6 large cloves garlic

1 pound beef

Salt and pepper, to taste

Directions:

Chop garlic cloves. Light and pre-heat grill. Place your chopped garlic in a large bowl and add the ground beef. Mix the garlic into the beef by hand and form into patties, evenly distributing the garlic into the beef. Place patties on grill and allow to fully cook.

Roast Turkey with Honey Cranberry Relish

Courtesy of the National Honey Board

(www.honey.com)

Serves 8

Ingredients:

1 medium orange

12 ounces fresh whole cranberries

¾ cup honey

2 pounds sliced, roasted turkey breast

Directions:

Quarter and slice unpeeled orange, removing seeds. Coarsely chop orange and cranberries. Place in medium saucepan and stir in honey. Bring to a boil over medium-high heat. Cook 3 to 4 minutes; cool. Serve over turkey.

VARIETIES OF GARLIC

- **Common, or Softneck, Garlic (Allium sativum):** Because this type of garlic lasts longest, it is the variety most commonly found in grocery stores. Despite being termed "softneck," common garlic's outer skin is much thicker than that of hardneck garlic, which increases its shelf life and allows it to be braided.

- **Hardneck Garlic (Allium sativum var. ophioscorodon):** In comparison to common garlic, hardneck garlic has a thicker neck but thinner skin. These bulbs can be either purple or white, depending on growing conditions.

- **Elephant Garlic (Allium ampeloprasum):** Recently named in 1941, elephant garlic is actually a leek which resembles a large garlic bulb. Although this garlic grows in larger portions, it is milder and lacks the health benefits of other garlic varieties.

Turkey Burgers with Cilantro Pesto

Serves 4

Ingredients:

Cilantro Pesto

1 clove garlic
1 cup cilantro leaves
¼ cup walnuts, chopped
¼ cup Parmesan cheese, grated
¼ teaspoon salt
¼ cup olive oil

Burgers

1 pound ground turkey
½ cup chopped onion
1 jalapeño pepper, seeded and minced
¼ cup prepared chunky salsa
1 clove garlic
½ teaspoon oregano
½ teaspoon salt
4 hamburger buns, split and toasted
Cilantro Pesto

Directions:

Cilantro Pesto

In a food processor, fitted with a metal chopping blade, with motor running, drop 1 clove garlic through feed tube to finely chop. Add 1 cup packed cilantro leaves, ¼ cup each chopped walnuts and grated Parmesan cheese, and ¼ teaspoon salt; process 45 to 50 seconds or until smooth, scrape down sides of bowl. With motor running, slowly add ¼ cup olive oil and process until well blended. Cover and refrigerate several hours. Makes ⅔ cup.

Burgers

In medium bowl, combine turkey, onion, jalapeño, salsa, garlic, oregano, and salt. Evenly divide mixture and shape into four burgers, approximately 4½ inches in diameter. Grill burgers over medium-high heat for 5 to 6 minutes per side until meat thermometer registers 160°F to 165°F and meat is no longer pink in the center. To serve, place cooked burgers on bun bottoms; top with 2 tablespoons Cilantro Pesto and bun tops.

"When tillage begins, other arts follow. The farmers, therefore, are the founders of human civilization."
—Daniel Webster

Honey Sweet and Sour Meatballs

Courtesy of the American Beekeeping Federation (ABF)

(www.abfnet.org)

Ingredients:

1- 1½ pounds ground beef

1½ teaspoons seasoning salt

¼ cup milk

½ teaspoon pepper

½ cup butter

½ cup honey

¼ cup wine vinegar

1 medium-sized onion, cut into
1-inch sections

2 tablespoons soy sauce

1 (8 oz.) can pineapple slices with juice

¼ teaspoon cayenne pepper, or to taste

2 tablespoons cornstarch

2 ounces water

Directions:

Combine beef with seasoning salt, milk, and pepper and mix thoroughly. Shape into meatballs and fry in oil or butter until browned well and completely cooked. In a large sauce pan, combine honey, vinegar, onion, soy sauce, and pineapple juice (set pineapple slices aside) and bring to a boil. Add cayenne and reduce to medium heat for three to five minutes. In a cup, combine cornstarch and water and mix until no lumps remain, then add to sauce to thicken. Place meatballs and pineapple slices in a serving dish and cover with sweet and sour sauce. Recipe can be doubled or tripled to serve more.

Pasta with Tomato Meat Sauce

Courtesy of the National Pasta Association

(www.Ilovepasta.com)

Serves 4–6

Ingredients:

1 pound pasta, uncooked

8 ounces lean ground beef

1 medium onion, chopped

2 cloves garlic, minced

6 large tomatoes, peeled, seeded, and diced

½–1 teaspoon salt

½ teaspoon dried oregano

½ teaspoon dried basil

½ teaspoon sugar

¼ cup red wine

Directions:

Prepare pasta according to package directions. While pasta is cooking, combine beef, onion, and garlic in a large skillet; cook until meat is no longer pink. Set aside. In blender, combine remaining ingredients; process for 30 seconds. Add tomato mixture to meat; simmer about 20 minutes. When pasta is done, drain well. Add the sauce to the pasta and serve.

Maple Thyme Marinated Hanger Steak

Courtesy of the New York State Maple Producers Association
(www.nysmaple.com)

Ingredients:

½ cup pure maple syrup
2 shallots, peeled and sliced
1 ounce fresh thyme
½ cup water
1 tablespoon kosher salt
1 teaspoon ground black pepper
2 pounds hanger steak

Directions:

Combine maple syrup, shallots, thyme, water, salt, and pepper and place in medium-sized flat container. Add hanger steak and marinate for 24 hours. Grill until desired temperature and doneness.

Grilled Steak with Pumpkin Puree

Serves 4

Ingredients:

4 beef sirloin steaks
4 medium potatoes, peeled and chopped
6 ounces pumpkin meat, chopped
1 tablespoon butter
¼ cup milk
Salt and pepper, to taste

Directions:

Place potatoes in a pan and cover with water. Bring to a boil over high heat. Reduce heat and simmer for 5 minutes. Add the chopped pumpkin and continue to cook for 15 to 20 minutes or until very tender. Strain and transfer to a bowl. Add the butter and milk. Mash with a potato masher and season to taste. Meanwhile preheat a grill. Lightly oil the rack of the grill. Brush oil over the steaks and season with pepper. Add the steaks to the rack and close the grill. Cook for 4 minutes then turn over. Cover and continue to cook for another 3 to 4 minutes for medium rare. Season with salt and serve immediately with the pumpkin puree.

Broiled Sirloin with Spicy Mustard and Apple Chutney

Courtesy of NHLBI, part of NIH and HHS

Ingredients:

Chutney

1 Granny Smith apple, rinsed, peeled, cored, and diced (about 1 cup)
2 tablespoons shallots, minced
1 tablespoon garlic, minced (about 2–3 cloves)
½ cup canned no-salt-added diced tomatoes
2 ounces golden seedless raisins (about ½ cup)
¼ cup apple cider vinegar
2 tablespoons pure maple syrup

Steak

4 (3 oz.) beef top sirloin steaks, lean
¼ teaspoon salt
¼ teaspoon ground black pepper
1 tablespoon olive oil

Mustard Dressing

2 cups low-sodium beef broth
2 tablespoons Dijon mustard
2 tablespoons cornstarch

Directions:

Chutney

Combine all the ingredients in a small saucepan. Bring to a boil over high heat, and simmer for 20 minutes or until apples are cooked and soft. Remove from the heat and hold warm, or cool and store.

Steak

Preheat grill pan or oven broiler (with the rack 3 inches from heat source) on high temperature. Season the steaks with salt and pepper, and lightly coat with oil. Grill or broil 3–4 minutes on each side, or to your desired doneness (to a minimum internal temperature of 145°F). Remove from the heat and set aside for 5 minutes.

Mustard Dressing

Mix together beef broth, Dijon mustard, and cornstarch in a small saucepan. Bring to a boil on medium-high heat while stirring constantly. Lower the heat, and simmer for 2–3 minutes. Serve each steak with ¼ cup of chutney and ½ cup of mustard dressing.

Braised Corned Beef with Maple

Courtesy of the Massachusetts Maple Producers Association

(www.massmaple.org)

Ingredients:

4 pounds premium corned beef, desalted
1 cup pure maple syrup
¼ cup bourbon (optional)

Directions:

Place desalted brisket on rack in roasting pan and bake uncovered at 325°F for 30 minutes. Reduce heat to 275°F, cover, and bake 2 hours. Uncover, discard all but ½ cup liquid, add maple and bourbon (if using), and continue baking and basting frequently for an additional hour. Save liquid as table sauce.

Roast Pork Loin with Apples and Cinnamon

Courtesy of the National Honey Board

(www.honey.com)

Ingredients:

1½ pounds boneless pork loin
1 tablespoon olive oil
1 teaspoon ground black pepper
1 teaspoon ground ginger
½ teaspoon nutmeg
½ teaspoon cinnamon

½ cup dry white table wine
1 tablespoon lemon juice
¼ cup honey
2 apples, cored, peeled and sliced into wedges

Directions:

Rub pork loin with olive oil, pepper, half of ginger, nutmeg, and cinnamon. Combine remaining half of spices with wine, lemon juice, and honey; stir in apple wedges. Preheat oven to 350°F.

Place pork in shallow baking pan. Roast to an internal temperature of 155°F, about 40 minutes. Remove from oven, cover and keep warm; let rest for 10-15 minutes. Reserve all juices.

Heat apple mixture to a boil. Reduce heat to a simmer. Cover and simmer until apples are tender, about 5 minutes. Add any pork juices, simmer a few minutes more. Remove from heat.

Slice pork loin; arrange on plates, pour warm sauce over slices, garnish with apples.

MEAT & POULTRY ENTREES

Pork Mignons with French Applesauce

Courtesy of NHLBI, part of NIH and HHS

Ingredients:

1 pair pork tenderloins (about 2 pounds)
¼ teaspoon salt
⅛ teaspoon ground black pepper
½ cup water
2 medium apples, rinsed and cored, but not peeled (try Golden Delicious or Rome)

2 tablespoons dark seedless raisins
2 tablespoons walnuts, broken into coarse pieces
½ teaspoon cinnamon
Cooking spray

Directions:

Preheat oven broiler on high temperature, with the rack 3 inches from heat source. Cover broiler pan with aluminum foil for easy cleanup. Spray foil lightly with cooking spray. Set aside.

Cut eight slices (pork rounds), each 1½-inch thick, from the center of the pair of pork tenderloins. Refrigerate or freeze the ends for another use. Place pork rounds on the foil-covered broiler pan. Sprinkle with salt and pepper. Set aside a few minutes while broiler heats.

Meanwhile, heat ½ cup water to boiling in a medium nonstick pan. Slice cored apples from top to bottom in ¼-inch wide pieces.

Add apples, raisins, walnuts, and cinnamon to boiling water. Reduce heat to medium. Cover. Simmer, stirring occasionally, until apples are soft and easily pierced with a fork. Set aside until pork is cooked.

Broil pork tenderloins for 5-10 minutes per side (for a minimum internal temperature of 160°F). To serve, place two pork rounds on each dinner plate. Top with ¼ of the applesauce.

Note: Also try doubling the sauce to serve over whole-wheat pancakes, or eat alone for dessert.

APPLES AS A GUILT-FREE SNACK

- Apples contain zero fat, cholesterol, or sodium.
- One medium apple is only about 80 calories.
- Most of the antioxidants and two-thirds of the fiber are found in the apple peel.

Baked Pork Chops with Apple Cranberry Sauce

Courtesy of NHLBI, part of NIH and HHS

Ingredients:

Pork Chops

4 boneless pork chops (about 3 ounces each)
¼ teaspoon ground black pepper
1 medium orange, rinsed, for ¼ teaspoon zest (use a grater to take a thin layer of skin off the orange; save the orange for garnish)
½ tablespoon olive oil

Sauce

¼ cup low-sodium chicken broth
1 medium apple, peeled and grated (about 1 cup) (use a grater to make thin layers of apple)
½ cinnamon stick (or ⅛ teaspoon ground cinnamon)
1 bay leaf
½ cup dried cranberries
½ cup 100% orange juice

Directions:

Pork Chops

Preheat oven to 350°F. Season pork chops with pepper and orange zest. In a large sauté pan, heat olive oil over medium heat. Add pork chops, and cook until browned on one side, about 2 minutes. Turn over and brown the second side, an additional 2 minutes. Remove pork chops from the pan, place them on a non-stick baking sheet, and put in the oven to cook for an additional 10 minutes (to a minimum internal temperature of 160°F).

Sauce

Add chicken broth to the sauté pan and stir to loosen the flavorful brown bits. Set aside for later. Meanwhile, place grated apples, cinnamon stick, and bay leaf in a small saucepan. Cook over medium heat until the apples begin to soften. Add cranberries, orange juice, and saved broth with flavorful brown bits. Bring to a boil, and then lower to a gentle simmer. Simmer for up to 10 minutes, or until the cranberries are plump and the apples are tender. Remove the cinnamon stick. Peel the orange used for the zest, and cut it into eight sections for garnish. Serve one pork chop with ¼ cup of sauce and two orange segments.

Note: A wonderful fruit sauce adds the perfect touch to these pork chops—try serving with a side of brown rice and steamed broccoli.

MEAT & POULTRY ENTREES

Spicy Maple Glazed Pork Chops

Courtesy of the New York State Maple Producers Association

(www.nysmaple.com)

Ingredients:

1½ cups pure maple syrup
½ cup white vinegar
¼ cup horseradish

2 tablespoons ancho chile powder
4–8 pork chops

Directions:

Preheat oven to 400°F. Mix maple syrup, vinegar, horseradish and chile powder well. Sear the pork chops on both sides, then place in a baking dish. Set aside half of the glaze. Baste the glaze over the chops and continue basting while the chops finish cooking. Pour the reserved glaze over the chops just before serving.

Honey Chinese BBQ Pork

Courtesy of Benefits of Honey, the number one ranked website on the health benefits of honey

(www.benefits-of-honey.com)

Ingredients:

2 pounds lean pork
2 cloves garlic, blended and ground
½ teaspoon five spices powder
1½ tablespoons soy sauce
½ teaspoon pepper

1 teaspoon salt
1 tablespoon margarine (or vegetable oil)
4-5 tablespoons honey (a rose honey variety works well)

Directions:

Slice pork thinly and tenderize slices. Add seasoning (garlic, five spices powder, soy sauce, pepper, and salt) and place pork slices in a container. Leave it in the refrigerator for at least 5 hours to marinate. Arrange thin pieces of pork on a flat plate to dry. When dry, cut pork slices into squares of about 4 inches. Barbecue the pork slices with burning charcoal until both sides are golden in color. Brush the slices with margarine (or vegetable oil) before grilling and glaze them with honey from time to time. Serve hot or store in the refrigerator for later use.

Stuffed Pork Tenderloin with Fresh Tomato Sauce

Courtesy of Carrie Balkcom, American Grassfed Association

(www.americangrassfed.org)

Serves 6–8

Ingredients:

Fresh Tomato Sauce

1¾ pounds Roma tomatoes (see note)

1 teaspoon olive oil

½ cup onion, diced

1 clove garlic, minced

½ cup tomato paste

2 cups chicken or vegetable stock (or more as needed)

2 tablespoons fresh basil, chopped

Salt and freshly ground black pepper, to taste

Pork

2 pork loins (about 4 pounds), trimmed

1 (4 oz.) log fresh goat cheese

3 tablespoons fresh rosemary, minced

2 tablespoons minced garlic

½ teaspoon salt

½ teaspoon freshly ground pepper

1 tablespoon olive oil

Rosemary sprigs, for garnish

Salt and freshly ground pepper, to taste

Directions:

Fresh Tomato Sauce

Peel, seed, and chop tomatoes. In large sauté pan that can be fitted with a lid, heat oil. Adjust temperature to medium heat, then add onions and garlic. Cover and sweat until soft, about 5 to 7 minutes. Add tomatoes and tomato paste and pincé over medium heat until rust-colored (see note). Add 1 cup of stock, stir, and cover pan. Simmer, stirring occasionally until sauce is thick, about 45 minutes (if sauce appears too thick during cooking time, add a little more stock to obtain desired consistency). Add basil and season with salt and pepper.

Pork

While Tomato Sauce is cooking, prepare pork loins. Preheat oven to 400°F. Cut each pork loin in half lengthwise, but not through one edge. Open the tenderloin like a book and spread half of the goat cheese along the inside of each loin. Season with salt and pepper. With a mortar and pestle, make a coarse paste of the minced rosemary, garlic, salt, and pepper. Spread over all sides of both pork loins. Tie loins with unwaxed string and allow to stand at room temperature for 30 minutes. Heat large oven-proof sauté pan over medium-high heat. Add olive oil and heat. Sear pork loins on all sides and transfer pan to preheated oven. Roast for 15 minutes for medium doneness. Remove from the oven and cover pan with foil. Allow meat to rest for 5 minutes before slicing. Slice loins about ½-inch thick and serve with Fresh Tomato Sauce strewn across the slices. Garnish with a few rosemary sprigs.

Note: If tomatoes are out of season, you can improve the flavor by roasting them if desired. Cut the tomatoes in half lengthwise, seed them, and place them cut-side up on a baking sheet. Roast in a 325°F oven for about 30 minutes. Remove skins and continue with the recipe.

Allowing tomato paste to pincé or "cook out" reduces the raw flavor (excessive sweetness, bitterness, or acidity) in the tomato paste. Tomato paste cooks out very quickly on the stovetop. Be careful not to burn.

MEAT & POULTRY ENTREES

Maple Baked Ham

Courtesy of Shaver-Hill Farm

(www.shaverhillfarm.com)

Ingredients:

2 teaspoons dry mustard
2 teaspoons lemon juice
¾ cup pure maple syrup
6–8 thick ham slices

Directions:

Mix mustard and lemon juice, and stir until smooth. Add maple syrup and pour over ham slices in baking pan. Bake uncovered at 350°F for 50 minutes, basting every 10 minutes.

Baked Fresh Tomato, Ham, and Swiss Rolls

Courtesy of the Florida Tomato Committee

(www.floridatomatoes.org)

Serves 4

Ingredients:

2 large fresh tomatoes (about 1 pound)
6 ounces sliced ham, cut in strips (about 1½ cups)
6 ounces Swiss cheese, shredded (1½ cups)
3 tablespoons creamy mustard blend
1 tablespoon prepared white horseradish
4 large, hard round (Kaiser) rolls, cut in halves

Directions:

Use tomatoes held at room temperature until fully ripe. Core tomatoes, cut in large chunks, and set aside. Preheat oven to 400°F. In a medium bowl combine the ham, cheese, mustard blend, and horseradish. Gently stir in the tomatoes. Remove the inside from the bottom portion of each roll, leaving ½- to ¾-inch thick shells. Place on a baking sheet. Fill each shell with about 1 cup of the tomato mixture and top with the upper portion of the roll. Bake until heated through and cheese starts to melt, about 15 minutes.

Roasted Duck with Currant Jelly Sauce

Ingredients:

Roast Duck

1 duck, washed and dried
6 cups bread crumbs
6 ounces butter
2 onions, chopped
1 teaspoon sage
1 teaspoon pepper
1 teaspoon salt
Water, salt, butter, and flour for basting

Currant Jelly Sauce

3 tablespoons butter
1 onion
1 tablespoon flour
1 bay leaf
1 sprig celery
1 pint poultry stock
2 tablespoons vinegar
½ cup currant jelly
Salt and pepper, to taste

Directions:

Roast Duck

Clean the duck thoroughly, and wipe dry. Cut the neck close to the back, beat the breast-bone flat with a rolling pin, and tie the wings and legs securely. In a bowl, mix together the bread crumbs, butter, onions, sage, pepper, and salt. Lightly stuff the bird with the dressing and sew up the openings to keep the flavor in and the fat out. Place in a baking pan, with a little water, and baste frequently with salt and water—you may also add onion and vinegar if you desire. Turn the duck often, so that the sides and back will be browned. When nearly done, baste with butter and a little flour. Young ducks should roast 25 to 30 minutes, and full-grown ones for about 1 hour, depending on size. Serve with the Currant Jelly Sauce.

Currant Jelly Sauce

Cook the butter and onion until the latter begins to color. Add the flour and herbs. Stir until brown; add the stock and vinegar, and simmer 20 minutes. Strain and skim off all the fat. Add the jelly and stir over heat until it is melted. Serve with roasted duck or turkey.

HEALTH BENEFITS OF BERRIES

The same pigments that give berries their vibrant hues of blues, purples, and reds also make them excellent for your health.

Berries contain high levels of phytonutrients—chemicals that are found in plants and believed to promote health. Since phytonutrients are most concentrated in the skin or peel of vegetables and fruits, berries are a great source due to their edible skins.

Shepherd's Pie

Courtesy of Hood River Garlic Farm

(www.hoodrivergarlic.com)

Serves 4

Ingredients:

Pie

1½ pounds organic ground beef

1 medium onion

2 carrots, peeled and chopped

1 tablespoon chopped garlic

1 tablespoon rosemary

½ cup chicken or beef stock

1 red or green pepper, chopped

1 tablespoon flour

Salt and pepper, to taste

Crust

2 quarts water

7 medium potatoes, chopped

3 tablespoons butter

3 tablespoons garlic

½ cup whole milk

Salt and pepper, to taste

Directions:

Pie

Pre-heat oven to 400°F. Heat ground beef in a skillet for about 10 to 12 minutes over medium heat, until cooked. Drain off fat. Combine onions, carrots, garlic and rosemary. Add chicken or beef stock and simmer about 12 minutes until carrots are tender. Add green pepper. Let all the soup stock evaporate, and mix in the flour. Make sure filling is moist but not too wet, drain off liquid if needed. Pour the pie mixture into an 8- x 13- x 2-inch deep baking dish. Set aside while preparing the crust mixture.

Crust

Bring two quarts of water to a boil. Add potatoes and boil until tender. Add salt, if desired. In a small skillet melt butter over low heat. Add garlic and stir frequently until the garlic is lightly brown. Drain off the potatoes, and transfer back into pot. Add milk and garlic and blend with mixer until all the lumps are gone. Salt and pepper to taste. Spread mashed potatoes over the meat mixture, making sure to cover the whole pie filling. Bake for 20 minutes, until crust is golden brown.

Perfect Honey Pizza

Courtesy of Benefits of Honey, the number one ranked website on the health benefits of honey
(www.benefits-of-honey.com)

Ingredients:

1-2 tablespoons honey (try Fireweed, Rewarewa or Tawari varieties)
5 slices soft white bread
3 tomatoes, finely chopped and drained
1 cup ham slices (cut into small 1- x 1-inch squares)

10 tablespoons shredded mozzarella cheese
Sesame, oregano, basil, pepper, thyme, and rosemary, to taste

Directions:

Spread honey on bread slices. Lay tomatoes pieces evenly on the bread, followed by ham squares. Spread cheese on top and finish off by sprinkling the mixed spices. Place in the oven at 285°F for 25-30 minutes.

Hot Hot Freezer Meatballs

Courtesy of the Garlic Seed Foundation
(www.garlicseedfoundation.info)

Ingredients:

1 egg
1 large head garlic cloves, peeled
1 small onion, sliced
¼ cup hot sauce (or less for less "heat")
1 pound lean ground beef
¾ cup quick cooking oatmeal
½ cup grated Parmesan cheese

1 teaspoon coarse ground black pepper
½ teaspoon salt (optional, cheese adds saltiness)
½ teaspoon Italian seasoning herbs (or ½ teaspoon each chopped fresh basil and oregano)

Directions:

Pre-heat oven to 400°F. Combine egg, garlic, onion, and hot sauce in a blender or food processor. Pour over meat in large bowl. Add the remaining ingredients and mix well with your hands. Scoop out 1-inch balls with melon baller or spoon onto large non-stick cookie sheet. Bake at 400°F for 15 minutes or until done. Time may vary depending on the size of meatballs and size of cookie sheet. Do not overcook or they will be too dry. Cool slightly, then pour off any fat, and/or drain meatballs briefly on paper towel. Cool completely; divide into meal-size portions for freezing.

Note: These make a versatile and quick meal in pasta or spaghetti sauce, in a quick sauce to put over potatoes, or in stir-fried vegetables (especially mixes of garlic and mushrooms).

VEGETARIAN ENTRÉES

Vegetarian entrées are meals prepared without using the flesh from fowl, fish, or meat. Instead, items like fresh fruits and vegetables, pasta, dry beans, lentils, nuts, tofu, tempeh, and other vegetarian substitutes are used to replace them.

Many people convert to a vegetarian lifestyle for health, economic, religious, or ecological reasons, or simply because they do not like the taste of meat. Some make a complete change and choose not to eat any meat at all. Others limit their meat intake to only poultry (pollo-vegetarians) or fish and seafood (pesco-vegetarians). Many people choose to practice casual vegetarianism and set aside a few days each week to consume only vegetarian meals. Even individuals who are not strict vegetarians can benefit from taking off days from eating meat and including vegetarian entrées in their weekly menus.

Vegetarian entrées certainly do not have to be poor tasting or bland meals. In fact, the smart use of spices and vegetarian items in recipes like A Honey of a Chili (page 105), Pasta with Tomatoes, Roasted Red Peppers, and Fresh Basil (page 109), or Mexibean Cheese Lasagna (page 106) will satisfy your appetite and your taste buds so completely that you may even find yourself forgetting that they are meatless meals. In this section, you will find the perfect blend of unique recipes and meatless twists on old favorite foods made with items available at your local farmstand, farmers market, or your own backyard garden to help keep your vegetarian meals inventive and flavorful every day of the week.

Cabbage and Pumpkin Stir-Fry

Serves 4

Ingredients:

2 teaspoons grapeseed oil
1 large onion, diced
1 garlic clove, minced
1 tablespoon minced ginger root
2 cups medium diced pumpkin meat
2 green onions, chopped
4 cups shredded purple cabbage

2 tablespoons low-sodium soy sauce
Cornstarch mixed with a little water
1 teaspoon sesame oil
1 tablespoon sesame seeds
Pepper, to taste

Directions:

In a wok, heat the grapeseed oil over medium-high heat. Add the onion and cook until translucent. Add garlic, ginger, and pumpkin, then stir-fry for 8 minutes. Add the green onion, cabbage, and a little water to avoid burning. Cook for 5 minutes or until the pumpkin is soft. Add soy sauce and gently mix. Thicken with cornstarch and water mixture. Drizzle with sesame oil, sprinkle sesame seeds, season with pepper, and serve immediately.

Celery and Apple Steam-Fry
with Honey-Mustard Sauce

Ingredients:

1 cup water
4 cups celery, diagonally sliced ½-inch thick
2 cups diced sweet red apples
(approximately 2 medium)
2 tablespoons Dijon-style mustard
1 tablespoon honey

1 teaspoon cornstarch
⅛ teaspoon ground black pepper
¼ cup chopped and toasted walnuts
(optional)

Directions:

In a large skillet bring water to a boil. Add celery and apples; cook and stir until crisp-tender, about 8 minutes. In a small bowl combine mustard, honey, cornstarch, and black pepper with 2 tablespoons of water. Add to celery mixture, stirring constantly; cook and stir until clear and thickened, about 1 minute. Stir in walnuts, if desired. Serve over rice.

Fruity Curried Lentils

Ingredients:
2 cups uncooked lentils
2 quarts water
2 apples cored peeled and chopped
¼ cup golden raisins
¼ cup non-fat lemon yogurt
1 teaspoon curry powder
½ teaspoon salt

Directions:
Combine lentils and water in a large saucepan. Bring to a boil over high heat. Reduce heat and simmer 20 minutes, stirring occasionally. Stir apples and raisins into saucepan; cook 10 minutes or until lentils are tender. Drain well. Place lentil mixture in large serving bowl. Stir in yogurt, curry powder, and salt until well blended.

Roasted Garlic and Winter Vegetables

Courtesy of Hood River Garlic Farm
(www.hoodrivergarlic.com)

Ingredients:
1 pound carrots, peeled
1 pound parsnips, peeled
1 large sweet potato, peeled
1 small butternut squash (about 2 pounds) peeled and seeded
1 bulb garlic, peeled (see note)
4 tablespoon extra-virgin olive oil

1 teaspoon sea salt
½ teaspoon fresh, ground black pepper
2 tablespoons chopped, fresh, flat-leaf parsley

Directions:
Pre-heat oven to 425°F. Cut the carrots, parsnips, sweet potato, and squash into 1- to 1¼-inch cubes (don't cut too small because they will shrink). Peel garlic but do not chop. Place vegetables into a large bowl, drizzle with olive oil, salt, and pepper; toss well. Transfer onto two sheet pans. Bake for 25-35 minutes, turning after the first 15 minutes. Test for doneness when all vegetables are tender. Sprinkle with parsley. Serve hot.

Note: A marbled purple stripe (like Siberian) or a porcelain (like Zemo) work well because of their large cloves.

Vegetables with Spicy Honey Peanut Sauce

Courtesy of the National Honey Board

(www.honey.com)

Ingredients:

½ cup honey

¼ cup peanut butter

2 tablespoons soy sauce

1 tablespoon chopped fresh cilantro

⅛ teaspoon crushed red pepper flakes

4 cups broccoli florets

4 cups sliced carrots

4 cups snow peas

6 cups cooked white rice

Directions:

Combine honey, peanut butter, soy sauce, cilantro, and red pepper in small bowl; mix well and set aside. Steam vegetables until crisp-tender; drain well. Toss steamed vegetables with peanut sauce in large bowl. Serve immediately over rice.

Spicy Grilled Tofu

Courtesy of the National Honey Board

(www.honey.com)

Ingredients:

1 (14 oz.) package extra firm tofu, drained and cut lengthwise into 8 slices

½ cup fresh lime juice

⅓ cup honey

¼ cup soy sauce

2 teaspoons chili paste with garlic

3 cloves garlic, minced (about 1 tablespoon)

¼ teaspoon ground black pepper

Directions:

Place tofu slices on several layers of paper towels; cover with additional paper towels. Let stand 20 minutes, pressing down occasionally with your hands to squeeze out water. Arrange tofu in single layer in 13- x 9-inch glass baking dish. Whisk together lime juice, honey, soy sauce, chili paste, garlic, and pepper in small bowl. Pour over tofu, coating each slice. Cover tightly with plastic wrap and chill 4 hours or overnight. Spray grill rack or pan with non-stick cooking spray. Heat grill or grill pan to medium heat. Remove tofu slices from baking dish, reserving marinade. Grill tofu slices 3 to 4 minutes on each side or until browned and crisp on the outside. Return tofu to baking dish and toss with reserved marinade. Serve immediately.

Stewed Pumpkin with Tomatoes

Ingredients:

3½ pounds pumpkin
1 medium-sized onion, chopped
1 quart stewed tomatoes, strained
1 tablespoon margarine
1 tablespoon cooking oil

1 tablespoon flour
¼ teaspoon pepper
2 teaspoons salt
Toast

Directions:

Wash and pare the pumpkin and cut into 2-inch square pieces. Parboil it for ten minutes. Using a stew-pan, fry the chopped onion until brown. Add the pumpkin, salt, and pepper, then cook for five minutes. Cover the pumpkin with the tomato, and stew gently until the pumpkin is quite tender. Arrange the pumpkin on a hot dish and thicken the tomato with margarine and flour cooked together. Add more seasoning if needed and pour the sauce over the pumpkin. Garnish with thin, narrow strips of toast.

Pumpkin Timbale

Ingredients:

1 pound pumpkin meat, diced small
1 tablespoon grapeseed oil
4 to 5 ounces ricotta cheese
1 teaspoon vanilla extract
Large pinch ground cardamom
Large pinch ground nutmeg
2 eggs
Salt and pepper, to taste

Directions:

Heat the oil and diced pumpkin in a pan over medium heat. Quickly sauté, cover, and reduce heat. Continue to cook for 10 minutes. Uncover and continue to cook over medium heat until the water is evaporated and the pumpkin very soft. Preheat the oven to 375°F. Prepare a warm "bain-marie" (water bath) for the oven. Transfer the pumpkin to a bowl and roughly mash. Add the ricotta cheese, vanilla extract, cardamom, nutmeg, eggs, a large pinch of salt, and pinch of pepper. Mash until well incorporated and then divide among four buttered ramekins. Place the ramekins in the warm bain-marie, making sure the water reaches only half of the height of the ramekins, and bake for 20 minutes.

VEGETARIAN ENTREES

Pumpkin in Ginger Coconut Sauce

Serves 4

Ingredients:

1 pound pumpkin meat, medium diced
1 tablespoon grapeseed oil
8 scallions, sliced
1 inch fresh ginger root, minced
1 jalapeño pepper, seeded and minced
1 (15 oz.) can unsweetened coconut milk

1 teaspoon red curry paste
2 tablespoons freshly minced cilantro
Salt and pepper, to taste

Directions:

Heat the oil in a saucepan over medium high heat. Add the pumpkin meat and sauté until slightly brown. Add the scallions, ginger, jalapeño, coconut milk, curry paste, cilantro, and bring to a boil. Reduce heat and continue to cook until the pumpkin is tender, about 15 minutes. Add a little water, if the milk thickens too much. Adjust seasoning and serve immediately.

Note: Try serving this dish over rice.

Chickpea, Tomato, and Spinach Curry

Serves 6

Ingredients:

1 cup onion, coarsely chopped
1½ tablespoons fresh ginger, chopped or grated
1 teaspoon olive oil
1½ teaspoons curry powder
1 (19 oz.) can chickpeas, rinsed and drained
1¾ cups tomatoes, chopped

1¼ cups fresh spinach, stems removed
½ cup water
¼ teaspoon salt (optional)

Directions:

Combine onion and ginger in food processor and pulse until minced. Heat oil in large skillet over medium-high heat. Add onion mixture and curry. Sauté for 3 minutes. Add chickpeas and tomatoes; simmer for 2 minutes. Stir in spinach, water, and salt. Cook another minute until spinach wilts. Try serving over brown rice.

Note: If you don't have a food processor, chop onion and ginger into small pieces.

Grilled Tofu Kabobs with Chipotle Marinade

Courtesy of the National Honey Board

(www.honey.com)

Ingredients:

Chipotle Marinade

1 cup vegetable broth
1 clove garlic, minced
⅓ cup honey
¼ cup tamari soy sauce
1 chipotle in adobo, minced
1½ tablespoons adobo sauce
1½ teaspoons granulated onion powder
1 tablespoon Dijon mustard
1 tablespoon fresh chopped cilantro

Grilled Tofu Kabobs

2 (14 oz.) packages extra firm tofu
2 cups Chipotle Marinade
3 medium zucchini, cut into
1-inch circles
1 medium red bell pepper, cut into 1-inch chunks
1 medium red onion, cut into
1-inch wedges
12 cherry tomatoes
1 cup pineapple cubes

Directions:

Marinade

Whisk together broth, garlic, honey, soy sauce, chipotle, and adobo sauce in 2-cup liquid measuring cup. Add onion powder, mustard, and cilantro; mix well.

Kabobs

Slice each block of tofu in half horizontally and, in a cross-hatch pattern, make two slices vertically and two slices horizontally for a total of 36 tofu cubes. Place tofu in a 9- x 13-inch baking dish. Pour marinade over tofu, cover, and refrigerate for 1 to 24 hours. Set and light fire using coals or mesquite about 30 minutes before cooking time. Soak bamboo skewers in hot water for 20 minutes. Alternating ingredients, thread tofu, vegetables, and pineapple cubes on skewers. Place kabobs over hot coals on well-oiled grill rack. Cook about 10 minutes, or until done, turning once and taking care that vegetables don't burn.

GRADES OF HONEY

When selecting honey at your local farmstand or farmers market, keep in mind that there are different grades of honey as well. Honey is classified as one of three quality grades: Grade A, Grade B, and Grade C. The grades, first established by the USDA back in 1985, are determined based on the honey's clarity, aroma, flavor, absence of defects, and water content.

Grade A honey is extracted honey that scores a minimum of 90 out of 100 points on the grading scale based on the determinants mentioned above.

Grade B honey must receive a minimum of 80 points.

Grade C honey scores at least 70 of 100 points. Any honey that receives less than 70 points on the scale is considered substandard grade.

Eggplant and Tomato Shish Kabobs with Pineapple, Sesame Rice, and Sweet Chili Sauce

Courtesy of www.ILoveEggplant.com

Ingredients:

Skewers

1 Japanese eggplant, stem ends removed, cut into 1-inch wedges

1 yellow squash, cut into 1-inch wedges

1 red bell pepper, cut into 1-inch by 1-inch sections

8 cherry tomatoes per serving

1 red onion, cut into 1-inch by 1-inch sections

8 button mushrooms

Mae Ploy™ Sweet Chili Sauce, for dipping

Directions:

Skewers

Stick alternating vegetables on skewers and set aside for grilling.

Rice

Next, place all rice ingredients in a small stockpot and bring to a simmer. Cover and turn the burner down to low heat. Cover the rice and let it cook for 20 minutes. Remove rice from heat, but keep covered until ready to serve. Grill the kabobs to your desired tenderness. When done grilling, serve the kabobs with the rice and the sweet chili sauce.

Note: If you are using wooden skewers, make sure to soak them in water overnight. This will help prevent them from burning on the grill.

Grape Kabobs with Yogurt

Serves 4

Ingredients:

Dip
1 cup chopped pineapple
¼ cup apple juice
¼ cup non-fat plain yogurt

Fruit
2 small bananas, cut into ½-inch thick slices
1 tablespoon orange juice
2 kiwifruits, peeled and cut into ½-inch thick slices
1 cup purple seedless grapes
⅓ cup small strawberries
⅓ cup melon balls
⅓ cup blackberries

Directions:

Dip
Bring the pineapple and apple juice to a boil in a small saucepan. Reduce the heat, cover, and simmer for 10 minutes, stirring occasionally. Let stand about 25 minutes or until cool. Transfer the pineapple mixture to a blender or food processor. Add the yogurt and blend or process until smooth. If desired, cover and chill in the refrigerator before serving.

Fruit
Place the bananas in a small bowl. Drizzle with the orange juice, then gently toss until coated. Cut the kiwi slices into quarters. For the kabobs, thread the grapes, bananas, kiwi, strawberries, melon balls, and blackberries onto 4-inch bamboo skewers. Serve with the dip.

TIPS FOR STORING BERRIES

- Do not store berries in their original container. Instead, remove and sort out any moldy or overripe ones. Then place the remaining berries in a loosely covered container.
- Do not wash berries until right before using them.
- Do not allow berries to sit in the sun or heat. Store them in a refrigerator set at 32°F - 40°F.
- For long-term storage, berries can be frozen in an airtight container. Those prepared without sugar should be used within 3 months. Berries prepared with sugar or any other sweetener can be kept for close to a year.
- Berries can also be pickled or preserved into a variety of jellies, jams, salsas, and chutneys.

VEGETARIAN ENTREES

Stuffed Sweet Peppers

Courtesy of the National Honey Board

(www.honey.com)

Ingredients:

1 tablespoon vegetable or olive oil

¾ cup uncooked long-grain rice

4 green onions, thinly sliced

¼ cup finely chopped fresh parsley

¼ teaspoon ground cinnamon

¼ teaspoon black pepper

¼ teaspoon salt

1 (14 ½ oz.) can vegetable broth

4 medium green bell peppers, cut lengthwise in half, seeded

1 (28 oz.) can crushed tomatoes in puree

¼ cup honey

½ teaspoon crushed red pepper flakes

1 (8¾ oz.) can garbanzo beans, drained

⅓ cup dried currants or raisins

Directions:

In large saucepan, heat oil over medium-high heat until hot; cook and stir rice, onion, and parsley 3 to 5 minutes or until rice begins to brown. Stir in cinnamon, pepper, and salt. Gradually add vegetable broth. Bring to a boil, reduce heat, cover, and simmer for 18 to 20 minutes or until liquid is absorbed and rice is cooked through. Meanwhile, cook green pepper halves in boiling water 5 to 7 minutes or until peppers are crisp-tender; drain. Combine tomatoes, honey, and crushed red pepper in 13- x 9-inch baking pan; mix well. Remove ¼ cup sauce; set aside. Arrange pepper halves on sauce in baking pan. When rice is cooked, remove from heat; stir in garbanzo beans, dried currants, and reserved ¼ cup sauce. Divide rice evenly among pepper halves in baking pan. Cover pan tightly with foil. Bake at 350°F for 30 minutes.

Roasted Garlic Grilled Cheese Sandwich

Courtesy of Peter McClusky, Toronto Garlic Festival

(www.torontogarlicfestival.ca)

Serves 1

Ingredients:

1 tablespoon roasted garlic puree (see recipe for Roasted Garlic Spread on page 169)

2 slices whole-wheat or multi-grain bread

2 slices cheddar, American, or Swiss cheese

1 tablespoon unsalted butter or any low-fat substitute

Directions:

Spread roasted garlic on a single side of one slice of bread. Place the cheese between the slices of bread so that the roasted garlic spread is on the inside. Spread butter on the outside of the sandwich and place in pan pre-heated to medium heat. When one side is golden, turn the sandwich and cook until light brown. Slice sandwich in half and garnish with a pickled garlic scape.

Note: Garlic scapes are delicious when pickled and can be served as a garnish with sandwiches or chopped and added to a salad or stir-fry.

A Honey of a Chili

Courtesy of the National Honey Board

(www.honey.com)

Ingredients:

1 (15 oz.) package firm tofu
1 tablespoon vegetable oil
1 cup chopped onion
¾ cup chopped green bell pepper
2 cloves garlic, finely chopped
2 tablespoons chili powder
1 teaspoon ground cumin
1 teaspoon salt
½ teaspoon dried oregano

½ teaspoon crushed red pepper flakes
1 (28 oz.) can diced tomatoes, undrained
1 (15 ½ oz.) can red kidney beans, undrained
1 (8 oz.) can tomato sauce
¼ cup honey
2 tablespoons red wine vinegar

Directions:

Using a cheese grater, shred tofu and freeze in zippered bag or airtight container. Thaw tofu, place in a strainer, and press out excess liquid. In large saucepan or Dutch oven, heat oil over medium-high heat until hot; cook and stir onion, green pepper, and garlic 3 to 5 minutes or until vegetables are tender and begin to brown. Stir in chili powder, cumin, salt, oregano, and crushed red pepper. Stir in tofu; cook and stir 1 minute. Stir in diced tomatoes, kidney beans, tomato sauce, honey, and vinegar. Bring to a boil; reduce heat and simmer, uncovered, 15 to 20 minutes, stirring occasionally.

Quick Spinach Casserole

Serves 8

Ingredients:

3 (10 oz.) boxes frozen spinach, thawed, rinsed and drained
2 cups non-fat cottage cheese
¾ cup egg substitute
¼ cup flour
½ teaspoon salt
3 tablespoons light buttery spread

Directions:

Mix all ingredients together and pour into a slow-cooker. Cover and cook on high for 1 hour. Reduce heat to low and cook for 4 more hours.

Spicy Apple-Filled Squash

Ingredients:

1 acorn squash (about 1 pound)
1 Golden Delicious apple, peeled, cored and sliced
2 teaspoons reduced-fat margarine, melted
2 teaspoons brown sugar

⅛ teaspoon cinnamon
⅛ teaspoon nutmeg
Dash ground cloves

Directions:

Heat oven to 350°F. Grease a 1-quart baking dish. Halve squash and remove seeds; cut into quarters. Place quarters, skin side up, in dish and cover; bake 30 minutes. Meanwhile, in medium bowl, combine apple, butter, brown sugar, cinnamon, nutmeg, and cloves. Turn cut sides of acorn squash up; top with apple mixture. Cover and bake 30 minutes longer or until apples are tender.

Microwave version: Halve and seed squash; cut into quarters. Arrange quarters, cut side up, in microwave-safe baking dish. Microwave on high (100 percent) 6 to 7 minutes, rotating squash halfway through cooking time. Top squash with apple mixture, cover with vented plastic wrap and microwave on high 4 to 5 minutes or until apples are tender.

Mexibean Cheese Lasagna
Serves 6

Ingredients:

2 teaspoons olive oil
1½ cups chopped onion
3 garlic cloves, minced
1 green pepper, coarsely chopped
1 red pepper, coarsely chopped
1 teaspoon ground cumin
2 teaspoons chili powder
⅛ teaspoon cayenne powder
1 cup frozen or fresh corn kernels

1 (15 oz.) can dark red kidney beans, rinsed and drained
1 (15 oz.) can black beans, rinsed and drained
1 cup no-added-salt tomato sauce
1 (4 oz.) can diced green chilies, drained
Non-stick cooking spray
6 corn tortillas
1 cup fat-free ricotta cheese
¾ cup low-fat cheddar cheese, shredded

Directions:

In large skillet, heat oil over medium high heat. Sauté onion, garlic, and peppers for 5 minutes. Stir in spices and sauté 1 additional minute. Remove from heat. Mix in corn, beans, tomato sauce, and diced green chilies. Spray 13- x 9-inch dish with cooking spray. Place three tortillas in the dish arranging to cover the bottom. Spoon in half of the corn mixture, and spread ½ cup ricotta cheese on top. Sprinkle with half of the cheddar cheese. Repeat layers, using up all the ingredients. Cook, uncovered at 350°F for 45 minutes, until casserole is thoroughly heated and cheddar cheese has melted. Let stand 5 minutes before serving.

Macaroni and Cheese

Ingredients:
4 cups macaroni
1 pound cheese, preferably sharp cheddar
2-4 tablespoons butter
1 tablespoon flour
1 cup milk
2 cups cream
Salt and paprika, to taste

Directions:
Break the macaroni into bits and drop into a large saucepan of rapidly boiling salted water. Boil macaroni until al dente. Drain. Have cheese grated about ½ hour before serving. Put a heaping tablespoon of butter into separate pan and heat slowly. Stir in flour, stirring constantly. When smooth and thick, add milk in increments. When it reaches boiling, add macaroni. Gradually add the cream and remainder of the butter. Add a generous dash of paprika and salt to taste. Just before serving, stir in the cheese, mix well; serve.

Pasta Primavera

Ingredients:
1 cup broccoli florets
1 cup sliced carrots
1 cup sliced zucchini
1 cup macaroni or rotini pasta

Sauce
1 tablespoon margarine
1 tablespoon flour
1 cup skim milk
¼ teaspoon dried basil
⅛ teaspoon black pepper
2 tablespoons Parmesan cheese

Directions:
Steam vegetables until crisp-tender, and cook macaroni according to package directions.

Sauce

In a small saucepan, melt margarine and blend in flour. Gradually stir in milk and seasoning. (Do not add cheese at this time.) Cook over medium heat, stirring constantly, until sauce thickens. Remove from heat and blend in cheese. Pour over hot vegetables. Add macaroni and mix together.

Bow Tie Pasta with Roasted Garlic and Eggplant

Serves 6

Ingredients:

1 bulb garlic, roasted

6 cups eggplant, peeled and cut into 1-inch cubes

½ cup balsamic vinegar

4 tablespoons olive oil

¼ teaspoon dried oregano

½ teaspoon fresh ground pepper

3 cups (about 3 medium) chopped tomatoes

1 (12 oz.) package dried large bow tie pasta

2 tablespoons fresh parsley

¼ cup freshly grated Parmesan cheese

Directions:

Separate roasted garlic cloves, peel, and set aside. In a medium bowl, combine eggplant, vinegar, 3 tablespoons olive oil, oregano, and pepper. Mix thoroughly and marinate in the refrigerator for 1 hour. Place eggplant mixture, with liquid, on a baking pan. Bake in a pre-heated 425°F oven for 25 minutes. Stir every 5 to 6 minutes. About 10 minutes before eggplant is completely cooked, heat remaining 1 tablespoon olive oil in a skillet. Add tomatoes and garlic. Sauté for 5 minutes. At the same time, cook pasta in a pot of boiling water according to package instructions. Drain and divide cooked pasta on four serving plates. Cover pasta with roasted eggplant. Cover with equal portions of tomato-garlic mixture and top with parsley. Serve immediately sprinkled with Parmesan cheese.

Thai Noodles with Tofu and Snow Peas

Courtesy of the National Honey Board

(www.honey.com)

Ingredients:

1 (15 oz.) package extra firm tofu, drained, pressed, and cut into ½-inch pieces

1 (9 oz.) package fresh Asian-style noodles

4 ounces snow peas, trimmed and diagonally cut

¼ cup chopped fresh cilantro

Marinade

⅓ cup rice vinegar

¼ cup honey

2 tablespoons peanut butter

2 tablespoons soy sauce

2 tablespoons vegetable oil

1 tablespoon sesame oil

2 cloves garlic, finely chopped

½ teaspoon crushed red pepper

¼ teaspoon ground ginger

Directions:

In a medium bowl, combine marinade ingredients. Add tofu; marinate 30 minutes. Cook noodles and snow peas in 3 quarts boiling water 1 to 2 minutes, or until peas are crisp-tender; drain. Rinse with cold water; drain. Place in a large bowl; add tofu and marinade. Toss gently to coat. Add cilantro; toss to coat.

Pasta with Tomatoes, Roasted Red Peppers, and Fresh Basil

Courtesy of the Central New York Tomatofest, from the kitchen of Melissa Gentilcore
(www.cnytomatofest.org)

Ingredients:

2 large red bell peppers
3 tablespoons olive oil
20 fresh medium Roma plum or multi-colored tomatoes
½ teaspoon salt
¼ teaspoon black pepper
1½ teaspoons sugar
6–8 medium garlic cloves, coarsely chopped
15 oil-cured olives, pitted and halved
20 fresh basil leaves, torn into pieces
1 pound pasta (rigatoni, shells or ziti)
1 (1 lb.) bag frozen spinach
¼ cup grated Pecorino Romano cheese

Directions:

Line broiler pan or cookie sheet with foil. Rub 2 tablespoons olive oil on red peppers and place them on the pan. Broil, turning frequently until all sides are blackened. Remove from broiler and wrap in aluminum foil. Set aside to cool. Preheat oven to 425°F. Cut tomatoes in quarters and place in a 9- x 13-inch baking dish. Sprinkle with salt, pepper, and sugar. Remove skin and seeds from cooled peppers and cut into large strips. Do not discard pepper juice. Add roasted red peppers with juice, chopped garlic, olives, and basil. Drizzle with 1 tablespoon olive oil. Bake for 25 minutes. While tomato mixture is baking, cook pasta and spinach according to package directions. Drain. Mix pasta and spinach together. Put pasta and spinach mixture in large serving dish. Top with baked tomato mixture. Sprinkle with grated cheese.

Spaghetti Squash with Fresh Tomato Sauce

Courtesy of Red Fire Farm

(www.redfirefarm.com)

Ingredients:

1 large spaghetti squash

2 onions, chopped

2 cloves garlic

1 red or green bell pepper, chopped

5 tomatoes, chopped

1 bunch basil

Olive oil

Grated Parmesan cheese, to taste

Salt and freshly ground pepper, to taste

Directions:

Cut squash in half lengthwise and scoop out the seeds. Place face down on a pan with ¼-inch of water and bake for 40 minutes at 350°F. While baking, start the sauce. In olive oil, sauté onions, garlic, and peppers for 5 minutes on medium heat. Add tomatoes, salt, and pepper to taste and simmer for the remainder of the squash prep time. Remove squash from the oven and stick a fork into the cut side. The fork should go in easily, but it should not be mushy. Cool for 5 minutes and use the fork to scrape the strands of squash from the skin, trying to keep them intact. Serve immediately topped with the sauce, fresh chopped basil, and cheese.

Okra with Rice, Tomatoes, and Beans

Ingredients:

½ cup chopped onions

2 cups chopped tomatoes

1 teaspoon sesame oil

1 cup sliced okra

2 cloves garlic, chopped

½ cup low-sodium vegetable broth

2 cups cooked brown rice

1 cup black beans, canned

Directions:

In a medium-sized saucepan, sauté the onions and tomatoes in the oil for 5 minutes. Add the okra, garlic, and broth. Cook for 15 to 20 minutes. Serve hot over the rice and beans.

Pizza with Sautéed Peppers, Onion and Garlic Scapes

Courtesy of Hood River Garlic Farm

(www.hoodrivergarlic.com)

Makes two pies

Ingredients:

Dough
3 tablespoons yeast (one packet)
1½ cups warm water
3 tablespoons olive oil
¼ cup white flour
¼ cup whole-wheat flour
1 teaspoon salt

Toppings
1 tablespoon extra-virgin olive oil
½ cup onion, diced
½ cup green pepper, diced
½ cup garlic scapes (about 6 scapes), cut into ¼-inch pieces
1 tablespoon flour
1 tablespoon corn meal
2 cups organic marinara sauce
2 cups shredded mozzarella cheese
¼ cup fresh basil, chopped into thin slices
Crushed red peppers, to taste

Directions:

Pre-heat oven to 400°F. In a sauce pan over medium heat, add olive oil. Allow oil to heat up. Add onions, peppers and scapes to oil. Sauté for five minutes, stirring frequently. Cook until tender. Set aside. Prepare your pizza dough as directed below. Place 1 tablespoon flour on small dish and roll pizza dough onto flour, then toss with fists. Put corn meal on pizza stone or cooking sheet. Carefully lay out pizza dough on stone. Add one cup marinara, one tablespoon at a time, evenly spreading over dough. Add one cup mozzarella, evenly spreading over marinara. Add half of garlic scape mixture, evenly spreading over cheese. Top with half the basil. Place in pre-heated oven for 18 to 22 minutes. Test center of pie for doneness. Remove from oven and transfer to cutting board. Let cool for 2 to 3 minutes before slicing. Garnish with crushed red peppers.

Dough

To prepare dough, place yeast in large mixing bowl and add warm water to dissolve, stir in olive oil. In another bowl, mix the salt and flours together and then knead them into the yeast mixture. Cover bowl with a towel and let rise for 30 to 40 minutes. Repeat using other half of ingredients.

VEGETARIAN ENTREES

Fresh Vegetable Pita Pizza

Courtesy of Florida Tomato Committee

(www.floridatomatoes.org)

Serves 4

Ingredients:

1 pound fresh tomatoes

4 (7-inch) pita breads

1 tablespoon olive oil

2 tablespoons grated

1½ teaspoons Italian seasoning, divided

2 cups shredded part-skim mozzarella cheese, divided

1 medium zucchini, cut in half lengthwise and thinly sliced (2 cups)

1 green pepper, thinly sliced

1 cup thinly sliced sweet red or white onion

Crushed red pepper, to taste

Parmesan cheese, to taste

Directions:

Preheat oven to 425°F. Use tomatoes held at room temperature until fully ripe. Core and slice tomatoes; cut each slice in half. Place pitas on two baking sheets; brush with oil. Arrange tomato slices on each pita, dividing evenly. Sprinkle with Parmesan cheese and half of the Italian seasoning. Bake until tomatoes are heated and pitas begin to crisp, about 10 minutes. Sprinkle tomatoes with half of the mozzarella cheese. Top with zucchini, green pepper, and onion. Sprinkle with remaining mozzarella and Italian seasoning. Bake until cheese is melted and vegetables are crisp-tender, about 10 minutes. Serve with crushed red pepper and additional Parmesan cheese, if desired.

"Cultivators of the earth are the most valuable citizens. They are the most vigorous, the most independent, the most virtuous and they are tied to their country and wedded to its liberty and interests by the most lasting bonds."

—Thomas Jefferson

Tomato and Romano Cheese Pie

Courtesy of Central New York Tomatofest, from the kitchen of Deborah Oliver

(www.cnytomatofest.org)

Serves 8

Ingredients:

5–6 medium tomatoes, peeled, sliced, and drained
1 lightly baked 9-inch pie shell
½–1 cup mayonnaise
½–1 cup grated pecorino Romano cheese
1 large clove garlic, minced
¼ teaspoon pepper
2 teaspoons dried (or 2 tablespoons fresh) basil
¼ cup Ritz® crackers, crushed
2 teaspoons melted butter
Salt, to taste

Directions:

Preheat oven to 350°F. Arrange tomato slices in pie shell. Blend all other ingredients except the crackers and butter. Spread over the sliced tomatoes. Mix cracker crumbs and melted butter. Sprinkle pie with the cracker/butter mix. Bake for 25-30 minutes.

HEALTH BENEFITS OF TOMATOES

Tomatoes are rich in antioxidants, especially vitamin C, betacarotene, manganese, and vitamin E. Antioxidants tame cancer-causing free radicals, and some studies suggest that tomatoes help fight cancer. The tomato's concentration of alpha-tomatine is especially effective in fighting prostate cancer.

SIDE DISHES

"We're having a last minute get-together at our house. It's just going to be a group of our close family and friends. We'd like you to come. We already have the main dish planned, so why don't you just bring a side dish that will go with it?" How many times have you received an invitation similar to this and instantly been stumped by what to make?

Whether they are prepared to serve your family at home or to share at a church or group potluck, party, barbecue, or other get-together, side dishes play an important role in meals. In fact, many meals are made up of a variety of side dishes. Since they normally consist of vegetables, fruits, beans, and grain items, side dishes help supplement entrées and provide nutritional balance to the meal.

Everyone seems to have their favorite standby dishes that have been tested and approved by their family and friends, but why not change things up next time and try one of these tasty sides? Instead of your typical side of mashed potatoes with your famous roasted turkey, next time surprise your guests with a complementary side of Cranberry Couscous (page 116) made with dried cranberries from your local farmers market. Show up at your next neighborhood barbecue with a side of Baked Beans with Maple and Rum (page 119) made with pure local maple syrup to complement the grilled meats, and you're sure to be a hit!

Cranberry Couscous

Courtesy of Cape Cod Cranberry Growers' Association, Carver, MA

(www.cranberries.org)

Serves 4

Ingredients:

2 tablespoons olive oil
¼ cup chopped white onion
½ cup sweetened dried cranberries
¼ cup chopped pistachios
1 cup couscous

1½ cups cranberry juice cocktail, heated to a simmer
2 scallions, green parts only
Salt and pepper, to taste

Directions:

In a medium saucepan add olive oil. Add the white onion, sweetened dried cranberries, and pistachios, then sauté gently over low heat until onion is translucent and slightly fragrant. Add the couscous and the warm cranberry juice cocktail. Stir with a fork to combine, cover. Let sit for 10 minutes. Add the scallions. Fluff with fork. Season to taste with salt and pepper. Toss gently to combine. Turn into serving dish. Serve hot.

Cranberry Risotto

Courtesy of Cape Cod Cranberry Growers' Association, Carver, MA

(www.cranberries.org)

Serves 8

Ingredients:

2 cups cranberry juice cocktail
2 tablespoons olive oil
¼ cup leeks, chopped
1 cup short grain white rice (such as Arborio)

¼ cup feta cheese, crumbled
½ cup sweetened dried cranberries
Salt and pepper, to taste

Directions:

Pour cranberry juice cocktail into small saucepan and place on medium-high heat. Bring to a boil. Add 2 tablespoons olive oil to 1–quart saucepan and place over high heat. Add leeks, salt, and pepper. Sauté until leeks are translucent and then add the rice. Stir until the rice is coated with oil. Add the boiling cranberry juice cocktail. Stir. Cover. Turn heat down to a simmer. Let simmer for 20 minutes. Remove from heat, add feta cheese and sweetened dried cranberries, then stir well. Turn into serving dish. Serve hot.

Brussels Sprouts with Pecans
and Dried Cranberries

Courtesy of the American Institute for Cancer Research

(www.aicr.org)

Ingredients:

1 (16 oz.) bag frozen, petit baby Brussels sprouts
1 tablespoon extra-virgin olive oil
2 teaspoon balsamic vinegar
2 tablespoons finely chopped, lightly toasted pecans

¼ cup dried cranberries
Salt and freshly ground black pepper, to taste

Directions:

Cook Brussels sprouts according to package directions. Meanwhile, in small bowl, stir together oil, vinegar, pecans, and cranberries. Transfer cooked sprouts to serving dish. Gently toss with dressing. Season with salt and pepper and serve immediately.

Roasted Pumpkin Seeds

Ingredients:

Pumpkin seeds
Olive oil (or melted butter)
Salt, to taste (optional)

Directions:

Remove the seeds from the pumpkin and place them in a bowl of warm water. Clean them gently to remove any excess flesh or strings. Drain the seeds in a colander, and lay them to dry on a towel. Once they are dry, heat the oven to 275-300°F. Place the seeds in a single layer on a baking pan, drizzle them with olive oil (or melted butter), and season them with salt (optional). Roast the pumpkin seeds for about 1 hour, stirring frequently. Allow them to cool. Store them in the refrigerator in an airtight container to maintain freshness.

Note: Pumpkin seeds may be roasted in the hull or can be removed first.

Roasted pumpkin seeds make an excellent healthy snack, salad topping, or nutty addition to many fish dishes.

Apple Stuffing

Ingredients:
½ pint unsweetened fresh applesauce
½ cup bread crumbs
Small chopped onion
Powdered sage, to taste
Cayenne pepper, to taste

Directions:
Mix together applesauce, bread crumbs, some powdered sage, and a little chopped onion, then season with cayenne pepper. Delicious for stuffing roast geese, ducks, Cornish hen, or turkey.

Simple Applesauce

Ingredients:
4 large apples, any variety, preferably sweet
½ cup water
½ teaspoon cinnamon

Directions:
Core, but do not peel apples; cut into chunks. Add apples to water and bring to boil. Reduce heat to low and simmer 25 minutes or until apples are soft. Add cinnamon and cook for 5 minutes. Cool. Place in blender and blend until smooth.

Note: Sweet apples will not require sugar. If tart apples are used, some sugar may be needed.

Broccoli with Pumpkin Hummus

Ingredients:
2 teaspoons flaxseed oil
1 tablespoon lemon juice
1 teaspoon ground cumin
½ teaspoon ground coriander
2 cups cooked garbanzo beans
2 cups cooked pumpkin purée
1 garlic clove, pureed
1 teaspoon paprika
3 pounds broccoli
Salt, to taste

Directions:
Combine all the ingredients, except the broccoli florets, in a food processor. Mix until very smooth and thin out with water as needed. Serve with broccoli florets.

Baked Beans with Maple and Rum

Courtesy of the Massachusetts Maple Producers Association

(www.massmaple.org)

Ingredients:

4 cups dry navy beans
3 quarts water
1 teaspoon baking soda
1 pound salt pork or ham
1 large onion
1 teaspoon dry mustard

1 cup pure maple syrup
1 tablespoon salt
4 apples, cored and unpeeled
1 cup pure maple sugar
½ cup butter
½ cup dark rum

Directions:

Rinse beans, cover with cold water, and soak overnight. Pour beans and water into large pot. Add baking soda and more water to cover beans. Bring to a boil uncovered and boil until some of the skins fall off when you blow on them. Line a bean pot with thin slices of the pork or ham, pour in beans and water. Roll onion in dry mustard until covered completely and bury it in the middle of the beans. Pour maple syrup and salt over top. Bake at 325°F for 4 to 5 hours. At the start of the last hour, place whole apples on top as close together as possible. Cream maple sugar and butter together and spread over top of apples. Pour rum over top just before serving.

Homemade Black Beans

Courtesy of Hood River Garlic Farm

(www.hoodrivergarlic.com)

Makes about 12 cups

Ingredients:

1½ pounds dry organic black beans
½ cup onion
1 tablespoon minced garlic

3 tablespoons organic molasses
1 teaspoon cinnamon
Salt and pepper, to taste

Directions:

The night before you want to make your beans, rinse the black beans well (be on the lookout for tiny foreign objects mixed in the beans, like small rocks!). Place the rinsed beans in a crock pot, fill with enough water to cover the beans (at least 1½ inches over the beans), and let sit over night. In the morning drain off the water and rinse again. Cover the beans with water again. Add the onion, garlic, salt, and pepper. Cover the crock pot and turn on high. Cook about 4 hours, stirring regularly. After the first 4 hours, test a bean to check for doneness. You can now turn the crock pot on low and continue to stir regularly until the beans are soft (they will probably take about 4 more hours on low). When they are cooked completely, turn off crock pot and stir in the molasses and cinnamon. Allow beans to sit until cooled. Set aside your 2 cups for the chili recipe (see page 78) and freeze the rest.

Tomato Tart

Courtesy of Central New York Tomatofest, from the kitchen of Linda Blanding
and Maryann Carriagan
(www.cnytomatofest.org)

Ingredients:

Pastry

1¾ cups flour
½ teaspoon salt
1 tablespoon sugar
¾ cup cold unsalted butter, cut in pieces
4 tablespoons ice water

Filling

¼ cup Dijon mustard
1 pound mozzarella cheese, thinly sliced
10 medium tomatoes, thinly sliced
1–2 tablespoons chopped garlic
1 teaspoon dried oregano
2 tablespoons olive oil
Salt and pepper, to taste

Directions:

Pastry

Combine flour, salt, and sugar in food processor. Add butter and combine until it reaches the consistency of a coarse crumble. With machine running, add water through the tube, processing until pastry rolls off the sides into a ball. Cover and refrigerate dough for 30 minutes. Roll out dough to fit tart pan or pie pan.

Filling

Preheat oven to 400°F. Brush mustard evenly over the bottom of pastry shell. Top the mustard with the mozzarella, completely covering the bottom. Arrange the tomato slices in overlapping concentric rings. Sprinkle top with garlic, oregano, salt, and pepper. Drizzle with olive oil. Put tart pan on baking sheet and bake for about 40 minutes.

SELECTING FRESH TOMATOES

For optimum taste, be sure to get tomatoes from your local farmstand in the summer and early fall. For maximum nutrients, choose richly colored tomatoes. Ripe tomatoes should exude a sweet aroma and be firm, yet yield slightly to pressure. Avoid buying tomatoes that are wrinkled, cracked, bruised, or puffy in appearance.

Pumpkins Squash
ORGANIC
50 ¢. LB
SCALE INSIDE

Scrumptious Grilled Vegetable Platter

Courtesy of www.ILoveEggplant.com

Ingredients:

3 tablespoons olive oil
¼ cup balsamic vinegar
1 teaspoon dried parsley
1 teaspoon dried oregano
½ teaspoon dried thyme
1 tablespoon minced garlic
1 teaspoon chicken bouillon
¼ teaspoon black pepper
2 tomatoes, cut in ½-inch slices

1 medium eggplant, cut into
½-inch rounds
2 cups Portabella mushrooms, sliced in
½-inch wedges
1 large zucchini, cut in ¼-inch slices
2 bell peppers, sliced in ½-inch strips
1 onion, cut in ½-inch rings

Directions:

Preheat grill to medium-high heat. Combine oil, vinegar, herbs, chicken bouillon, and pepper in a bowl and mix well. Add vegetables, mixing well to ensure all are coated with the marinade. Let stand for 30 minutes, mixing occasionally. Arrange vegetable pieces on the grill, reserving leftover marinade in bowl. Keep turning every 4–5 minutes until cooked on both sides, brushing with leftover marinade as they cook. Serve as an appetizer or as a vegetable side with your favorite pasta.

Artichoke Gondolas

Serves 4

Ingredients:

4 medium-sized artichokes, cooked
½ cup sun-dried tomatoes (not oil-packed)
1 small eggplant, peeled and diced
2 cups low-sodium chicken broth
¼ cup chopped onion

1 tablespoon fresh oregano
1 tablespoon fresh basil
2 cloves garlic, minced
¼ teaspoon pepper

Directions:

Halve artichokes lengthwise; remove center petals and fuzzy centers of artichokes. Remove outer leaves of artichokes; reserve. Trim out hearts and chop finely. Set aside. Rehydrate tomatoes in boiling water for 3 minutes until softened. Drain and rinse; chop. Cook eggplant in simmering chicken broth for 10 minutes; drain well. In blender or food processor container, place chopped tomatoes, drained eggplant, onion, herbs, garlic, salt, and pepper. Cover and process until nearly smooth. Taste for seasoning. Stir in chopped artichoke hearts. To serve, arrange artichoke leaves on a serving platter; spoon one heaping teaspoon of the eggplant mixture onto wide end of artichoke leaves. Garnish with a fresh herb leaf, if desired. Alternate serving idea: Arrange artichoke leaves on a platter, surrounding a bowl of the eggplant mixture. Use artichoke leaves to scoop up individual servings of the dip. Dip can be prepared up to 24 hours ahead and chilled until serving time.

Rosemary Potato Skewers

Serves 4

Ingredients:

4 medium red potatoes (about 1⅓ pounds) peeled and cut into 1½-inch chunks

1 tablespoon olive oil

2 teaspoons butter, melted

1 tablespoon chopped, fresh rosemary or 1 teaspoon dried rosemary

1 large clove garlic, minced

½ teaspoon salt

¼ teaspoon ground black pepper

4 (12-inch) skewers (metal or bamboo), soaked in warm water for 30 minutes

Directions:

Prepare a charcoal grill or pre-heat broiler. In a heavy saucepan with tight-fitting lid, cook the potatoes in 2 inches of boiling water until tender, approximately 15 minutes. Drain potatoes; cool slightly and thread onto skewers. In a small bowl, mix together remaining ingredients. Place potato skewers on the grill 3 to 4 inches above the glowing embers. Brush the skewers with the rosemary mixture. Grill, basting and turning several times, until the potatoes are lightly browned, approximately 10 to 12 minutes.

Sweet Pickle Relish

Makes 8 half-pint jars

Ingredients:

1 quart chopped cucumbers

2 cups chopped onions

1 cup chopped green peppers

1 cup chopped red peppers

¼ cup salt

3½ cups sugar

1 tablespoon celery seed

1 tablespoon mustard seed

2 cups distilled white vinegar

Directions:

Prepare jars, lids, and hot water bath canner according to manufacturer instructions.

Combine cucumbers, onions, peppers, and salt in a large glass or stainless steel bowl. Cover with cold water and set aside for 2 hours. Drain and rinse thoroughly.

Combine sugar, spices, and vinegar in a large stainless steel saucepan; bring to a boil over medium heat. Add drained and rinsed vegetables, then return to a boil and simmer for 10 minutes, stirring occasionally.

Pack hot relish into hot prepared jars, leaving ¼ inch head space at the top of each jar. Wipe the outer rim of the jars with a clean damp cloth to ensure a tight fit. Adjust the two-piece lids and secure snugly.

Place jars in hot water bath canner, making sure the water covers the jars by at least 1 inch. Boil for 10 minutes. Turn heat off, remove jars, and cool overnight. Remove outer lid and store.

Sauerkraut
Makes 12 pints or 6 quarts

Ingredients:

25 pounds cabbage
1 cup canning salt

Directions:

Remove outer leaves from firm cabbage heads; wash and drain. Cut into halves or quarters and remove the core. Use a shredder to cut cabbage into thin shreds.

Combine 5 pounds of shredded cabbage with 3 tablespoons of canning salt in a large glass bowl. Let salted cabbage stand for 10 minutes so that it wilts slightly. Pack salted cabbage into a large pickling container and press down firmly with a clean wooden spoon or clean hands, until cabbage juice comes to the surface. Repeat this step until all cabbage is in the pickling container. If juice does not cover the cabbage, add brine (see note below).

Place a large clean inverted plate with weights on top (such as sterile filled quart jars) over the cabbage to keep the cabbage 2 to 4 inches below the brine. Cover with a clean towel and place in a cool place.

The cabbage must be fermented, a process that takes up to 6 weeks. Each day, check the cabbage and skim off any foam that has formed and ensure the cabbage is still below the brine. Gas bubbles may also form during fermentation, but will cease once fermentation is complete.

Prepare jars, lids, and hot water bath canner according to manufacturer instructions.

Pack sauerkraut with brine into hot prepared jars, leaving 1/2 inch head space at the top of each jar. Wipe the outer rim of the jars with a clean damp cloth to ensure a tight fit. Adjust the two-piece lids and secure snugly.

Place jars in hot water bath canner, making sure the water covers the jars by at least 1 inch. Boil for 20 minutes for pint jars or 30 minutes for quart jars. Turn heat off, remove jars, and cool overnight. Remove outer lid and store.

Note: To make brine, combine 4 ½ teaspoons of canning salt with 4 cups of water; bring to a boil over medium-high heat to dissolve the salt. Let cool to room temperature; ladle over cabbage to cover.

SIDE DISHES

Chow-Chow Relish

Makes 4 pints

Ingredients:

1 quart chopped cabbage
3 cups diced cauliflower
2 cups chopped green tomatoes
2 cups chopped green peppers
1 cup chopped red peppers
3 tablespoons salt
1 ½ cups sugar

2 teaspoons celery seed
2 teaspoons dry mustard
1 teaspoon turmeric
½ teaspoon ginger
2½ cups distilled white vinegar

Directions:

Combine vegetables in a large glass or stainless steel bowl. Cover with water and salt, then set aside for 6 hours. Drain and rinse thoroughly.

Prepare jars, lids, and hot water bath canner according to manufacturer instructions.

Combine sugar, spices, and vinegar in a large stainless steel saucepan; bring to a boil over medium-high heat. Add drained and rinsed vegetables, then simmer for 10 minutes. Bring to a full boil again, lower heat, and simmer for another 10 minutes.

Pack mixture into hot prepared jars, leaving ¼ inch head space at the top of each jar. Wipe the outer rim of the jars with a clean damp cloth to ensure a tight fit. Adjust the two-piece lids and secure snugly.

Place jars in hot water bath canner, making sure the water covers the jars by at least 1 inch. Boil for 10 minutes. Turn heat off, remove jars, and cool overnight. Remove outer lid and store.

Oriental Honey Pickles

Courtesy of Benefits of Honey, the number one ranked website on the
health benefits of honey
(www.benefits-of-honey.com)

Ingredients:

Pickling Syrup

6-7 tablespoons lemon juice (substitute
4-5 tablespoons white vinegar for stronger
pickles, or use a mixture of lemon juice and
vinegar if you prefer)

2 tablespoons honey (a light, mild floral
variety)

4 tablespoons water

2 teaspoons sea salt

Pickles

1 small carrot

½ small turnip

½ cucumber

2 slices Chinese cabbage

1-2 long red chili peppers

½ slice pineapple (not too ripe)

1 tablespoon roasted sesame seeds

1 tablespoon ground roasted peanuts
(optional)

Directions:

Pickling Syrup

Mix together the lemon juice, honey, water, and sea salt in a bowl and set aside.

Pickles

Wash all vegetables. Remove seeds from cucumber and chili peppers. Cut carrot, turnip,
cucumber, cabbage, and chili peppers into thin strips about 2 inches long. Cut the pineapple
into small, thin sections. Mix the pickling syrup, sesame seeds, and peanuts (optional) into
the vegetables and pack them into a glass jar. Enjoy immediately or store in refrigerator for
stronger- tasting pickles.

Note: It is difficult to specify the amount of vegetables needed due to the odd sizes they
may come in. Therefore, you may have to do some adjustments in terms of the amount of
pickling syrup that you prepare.

HEALTH BENEFITS OF HONEY

Since honey is a natural source of carbohydrates, it is an excellent way to boost
energy levels. In fact, it is often used by athletes to boost performance and reduce
muscle fatigue during exercise. The glucose found in honey is a natural sugar
that the body absorbs quickly, so it provides a quick boost of energy. Fructose, the
other main natural sugar found in honey, is absorbed into the body more slowly
and provides sustained energy.

Pickled Green Beans

Makes 4 pints

Ingredients:

2 pounds green beans
¼ cup canning salt
2½ cups distilled white vinegar

2½ cups water
4 cloves garlic
4 dill heads

Directions:

Prepare jars, lids, and hot water bath canner according to manufacturer instructions.

Wash and trim ends of green beans. Combine salt, vinegar, and water in a stainless steel saucepan; bring to a boil over medium heat.

Pack raw green beans into hot prepared jars, leaving ¼ inch head space at the top of each jar. To each pint jar, add 1 clove of garlic and 1 dill head. Using a ladle and a funnel, pour the hot mixture over packed green beans, leaving ¼ inch head space. Wipe the outer rim of the jars with a clean damp cloth to ensure a tight fit. Adjust the two-piece lids and secure snugly.

Place jars in hot water bath canner, making sure the water covers the jars by at least 1 inch. Boil for 10 minutes. Turn heat off, remove jars, and cool overnight. Remove outer lid and store.

Pickled Green Tomatoes

Makes 6 pints

Ingredients:

5 pounds green tomatoes, small, firm, and unblemished
¼ cup canning salt
3½ cups distilled white vinegar

3½ cups water
6 cloves garlic
6 dill heads
6 bay leaves

Directions:

Prepare jars, lids, and hot water bath canner according to manufacturer instructions.

Wash and core the green tomatoes. Combine salt, vinegar, and water in a large stainless steel saucepan; bring to a boil over medium heat.

Pack raw green tomatoes into hot prepared jars, leaving ¼ inch head space at the top of each jar. To each pint jar, add 1 clove of garlic, 1 dill head, and 1 bay leaf. Using a ladle and a funnel, pour the hot mixture over packed green tomatoes, leaving ¼ inch head space. Wipe the outer rim of the jars with a clean damp cloth to ensure a tight fit. Adjust the two-piece lids and secure snugly.

Place jars in hot water bath canner, making sure the water covers the jars by at least 1 inch. Boil for 15 minutes. Turn heat off, remove jars, and cool overnight. Remove outer lid and store.

Pickled Garlic

Courtesy of the Garlic Seed Foundation
(www.garlicseedfoundation.info)

Ingredients:

5 cloves garlic
½ cup pickling salt
4 cups cracked ice
5 cups sugar
5 cups vinegar
1½ teaspoons turmeric

½ teaspoon cloves
2 tablespoons mustard seed
2 tablespoons celery seed
6 (pint-sized) canning jars and lids

Directions:

Peel garlic, sprinkle with salt. Bury garlic in 4 cups cracked ice. Cover with heavy plate. Let stand 3 hours to overnight, then drain. Combine garlic, sugar, vinegar, turmeric, cloves, mustard seed, and celery seed in a pan and bring to a boil. Meanwhile, sterilize canning jars and lids in boiling water. Pour garlic and liquid mixture into hot jars and seal. Let sit for at least one month.

Baked Cinnamon-Sugar Pumpkin

Ingredients:

1 medium pumpkin, peeled and sliced ¼-inch thick
Butter, as needed
Sugar and cinnamon, to taste

Directions:

Place a layer of pumpkin in the bottom of a baking dish, followed by a layer of sugar with a sprinkle of cinnamon and a dot of butter. Repeat until the pan is full. The top should be well covered with sugar. Bake in the oven on medium heat until the sugar becomes like a thick syrup.

Spiced Apples

Ingredients:

6 medium apples, peeled and pared
1 cinnamon stick, broken into pieces
4 cloves
2 cloves allspice
2 blades mace
½ teaspoon nutmeg
¾ cup brown sugar
½ cup apple cider

Directions:

Place peeled and pared apples in a casserole and then the stick of cinnamon, broken into pieces. Add cloves, allspice, blades of mace, nutmeg, brown sugar, and cider. Bake at 350°F for 30 to 40 minutes or until tender and allow to cool. Serve them cold.

Maple Glazed Vegetables

Courtesy of Shaver-Hill Farm
(www.shaverhillfarm.com)

Ingredients:

1 winter squash
1 sweet potato
3 carrots
Pure maple syrup, to cover

Directions:

Wash winter squash, sweet potato, and carrots. Slice lengthwise. Boil or steam until fork tender. Drain and place in shallow skillet. Pour on enough maple syrup to cover bottom of pan. Thin syrup by adding a small amount of water. Stir. Dot veggies with butter and cook uncovered in 300°F oven, or on top of stove at medium heat until glazed. Baste every 5 minutes.

Maple-Glazed Butternut Squash

Courtesy of the Massachusetts Maple Producers Association

(www.massmaple.org)

Ingredients:

1 medium butternut squash, peeled, seeded, cut into ½ –inch slices
4 tablespoons pure maple syrup
¼ teaspoon ground mace
4 tablespoons dark rum
⅔ cup water

Directions:

Place all ingredients in a large saucepan. Bring to a boil, then simmer for 15 minutes, or until the squash is tender. Reserving the cooking liquid, transfer the squash with a slotted spoon to a heated serving dish. Boil the cooking liquid until it is thickened, then pour it over the squash.

Poached Figs with Honey and Red Wine Sauce

Ingredients:

1 cup dry red wine
2 tablespoons flour
¼ cup honey
2 sticks cinnamon
7-8 fresh figs

Directions:

Pour the wine into a pan and add the flour. Allow the flour to dissolve and then warm the mixture over medium heat. In a separate saucepan, warm the honey until it reaches a syrupy consistency. Add the warmed honey and cinnamon sticks to the wine mixture. Heat the mixture on medium-low for another 7 to 8 minutes. Turn the burner down to low and add the figs, standing them up straight in the pan. Place a lid on the pan and allow to cook until figs are fully cooked, stirring occasionally. The figs should take approximately 20 minutes to cook. Before serving, remove the cinnamon sticks from the pan. Neatly place the figs in individual bowls and drizzle the honey and red wine sauce over the top. Serve while hot.

Pickled Hot Peppers

Makes 5 pints

Ingredients:

1 pound jalapeño peppers
1½ pounds banana peppers
¼ pound serrano peppers
6 cups distilled white vinegar
2 cups water
3 cloves crushed garlic

Directions:

Prepare jars, lids, and hot water bath canner according to manufacturer instructions.

Wash peppers, drain. Leave the peppers whole or cut them into 1-inch pieces. Mix peppers together. Combine vinegar, water, and garlic in a large stainless steel saucepan. Bring to a boil over medium-high heat. Reduce heat and simmer for 5 minutes. Strain out the garlic.

Using a ladle and a funnel, pack the peppers and hot liquid into hot prepared jars, leaving ¼ inch head space at the top of each jar. Wipe the outer rim of the jars with a clean damp cloth to ensure a tight fit. Adjust the two-piece lids and secure snugly.

Place jars in hot water bath canner, making sure the water covers the jars by at least 1 inch. Boil for 10 minutes. Turn heat off, remove jars, and cool overnight. Remove outer lid and store.

Note: Always wear gloves while handling or cutting hot peppers. If you do not wear gloves, be sure to wash your hands thoroughly with soap and water before touching your face or eyes.

Honey Candied Sweet Potatoes

Courtesy of Bees-And-Beekeeping.com

Ingredients:

¾ cup honey
2 tablespoons shortening
¼ teaspoon mace
¼ teaspoon cinnamon
6 sweet potatoes, boiled and peeled

Directions:

Mix the honey, shortening, mace, and cinnamon in a large frying pan. Bring to a boil and cook until the mixture thickens. Place the sweet potatoes and 4 tablespoons of water into the honey syrup and turn potatoes frequently, coating well with the syrup. Cook the potatoes under low heat for 20 minutes.

HONEY: A HEALTHY TREAT

- One tablespoon of honey contains 64 calories and 17 grams of carbohydrates.
- Honey contains antioxidants that fight cholesterol and have the potential to protect against heart disease.
- Darker honeys usually have higher antioxidant content than lighter honeys do.

BEVERAGES

Beverages provide cold relief on hot days. They also do an excellent job of warming up chilled bodies during cold weather. They soothe, refresh, replenish, and provide nourishment when needed. Some are hot, some cold. Some contain fresh fruit, while others are made with vegetables. Some beverages contain alcohol and are strictly for adults, while others are made of tasty ingredients that are equally pleasing for kids and grownups alike.

On a hot sunny day, lounge on your front lawn with a refreshing glass of iced Apple Juice (page 136) made fresh from apples plucked from your local apple orchard or found at your farmers market. On a cold winter afternoon, curl up by the fireplace with a loved one and a warm Apple Toddy (page 138) or a large mug of Magic Mint Hot Chocolate (page 140).

Whether you're looking for a breakfast drink, a smoothie or a vegetable-based beverage to supplement your meal, a festive punch to serve your friends at your next party, a milkshake to enjoy as a treat, or a beverage to simply refresh you, this section has a drink recipe to meet every occasion or need.

Apple Punch

Ingredients:
Apples, sliced
Lemons, sliced
Powdered sugar
1 bottle claret

Directions:
Slice apples and lemons and lay in alternate layers in a china bowl, covering each layer thickly with powdered sugar, until the bowl is about half filled. Pour a bottle of claret over it and let stand six hours. After pouring through a muslin bag, it is ready for use.

Raspberry Punch

Ingredients:
1 pint raspberries, washed
½ cup water
1½ cups sugar
½ cup maraschino cherries, chopped fine
Juice from small bottle of cherries
Lemon juice
Crushed ice
Carbonated water

Directions:
Place raspberries, water, and sugar in a saucepan and bring to a slow boil. When fruit is soft, rub it through a fine sieve and add the maraschino cherries and the cherry juice. To serve, place ½ cup of the prepared raspberry syrup in a tall glass and add 1 tablespoon of lemon juice, ½ cup of crushed ice, and fill the rest of the way with carbonated water.

Honey Punch

Courtesy of the American Beekeeping Federation (ABF)

(www.abfnet.org)

Ingredients:

1 cup honey

½ cup hot water

½ cup lemon juice

1½ cups orange juice

1 (46 oz.) can unsweetened pineapple juice

1½ cups cold water

1-2 liters ginger ale

Lemon or orange slices and maraschino cherries, for garnish

Directions:

Add honey to hot water; add fruit juices and cold water. Chill. Just before serving, add ginger ale. Garnish with lemon or orange slices and maraschino cherries.

Maple Fruit Punch

Courtesy of Shaver-Hill Farm

(www.shaverhillfarm.com)

Ingredients:

2 cups pure maple syrup

2 cups strawberry pieces (or other fruit)

1 cup orange juice

¾ cup crushed pineapple

2 cups strong tea

½ cup lemon juice

Directions:

Mix ingredients and chill for 1 hour. Add water or soda water to make one gallon of punch.

Tomato Juice

Makes 6 quarts

Ingredients:
25 pounds tomatoes, about 4 pounds per quart
Bottled lemon juice (approximately 12 tablespoons)

Directions:
Prepare jars, lids, and hot water bath canner according to manufacturer instructions.

Wash tomatoes and remove the cores. Cut tomatoes in quarters and place in a large stainless steel saucepan. Cook the tomatoes on low to medium heat until they are soft, stirring frequently to prevent sticking. Juice the tomatoes in a food mill or food processor.

Strain tomatoes; discard seeds and skins. Place the juice in a large stainless steel saucepan. Heat the mixture for about 5 minutes or until the juice temperature reaches 190°F; do not boil. Using a ladle and a funnel, spoon the hot juice into prepared hot jars. Add 2 tablespoons of lemon juice to each quart jar of tomato juice. Leave ¼ inch head space from the top of each jar. Wipe the outer rim of the jars with a clean damp cloth to ensure a tight fit. Adjust the two-piece lids and secure snugly.

Place jars in hot water bath canner, making sure the water covers the jars by at least 1 inch. Boil for 40 minutes. Turn heat off, remove jars, and cool overnight. Remove outer lid and store.

Note: For this recipe, you can vary the amount of lemon juice to make more or less than indicated. A good rule of thumb to follow is to use 2 tablespoons per quart.

Apple Juice

Makes 6 quarts

Ingredients:
25 pounds apples, about 75 medium apples
2 quarts water

Directions:
Prepare jars, lids, and hot water bath canner according to manufacturer instructions. Wash, stem, and chop apples. Place apples in a large stainless steel saucepan; add water. Cook the apples until they are tender. Strain apples in a damp jelly bag (or several layers of cheese cloth in a colander). Once all of the juice has dripped into a large stainless steel saucepan, heat the mixture for about 5 minutes or until the juice temperature reaches 190°F; do not boil. Using a ladle and a funnel, spoon the hot juice into prepared hot jars. Leave ¼ inch head space from the top of each jar. Wipe the outer rim of the jars with a clean damp cloth to ensure a tight fit. Adjust the two-piece lids and secure snugly.

Place jars in hot water bath canner, making sure the water covers the jars by at least 1 inch. Boil for 10 minutes. Turn heat off, remove jars, and cool overnight. Remove outer lid and store.

Tomato Vegetable Juice
Makes 7 quarts

Ingredients:

25 pounds tomatoes, about 4 pounds per quart
¼ cup chopped parsley
1 cup diced carrots
1 cup chopped celery

1 cup chopped green peppers
½ cup chopped onions 1 tablespoon salt
Bottled lemon juice (approximately 14 tablespoons)

Directions:

Prepare jars, lids, and hot water bath canner according to manufacturer instructions.

Wash tomatoes and remove the cores. Cut tomatoes in quarters. Place tomatoes, parsley, and vegetables in a large stainless steel saucepan. Cook the tomatoes and vegetables on medium-low heat until they are soft, about 20 minutes. Stir occasionally to prevent sticking. Juice the mixture in a food mill or food processor.

Strain, discarding seeds and skins. Place the juice in a large stainless steel saucepan. Stir in salt and heat this for about 5 minutes or until the juice temperature reaches 190°F; do not boil. Ladle hot juice into prepared hot jars. Add 2 tablespoons of lemon juice to each quart jar. Leave ¼ inch head space from the top of each jar. Wipe the outer rim of the jars with a clean damp cloth to ensure a tight fit. Adjust the two-piece lids and secure snugly.

Place jars in hot water bath canner, making sure the water covers the jars by at least 1 inch. Boil for 40 minutes. Turn heat off, remove jars, and cool overnight. Remove outer lid and store.

Note: For this recipe, you can vary the amount of lemon juice to make more or less than indicated. A good rule of thumb to follow is to use 2 tablespoons per quart.

Hot Honey Cider
Courtesy of the National Honey Board
(www.honey.com)

Ingredients:

1 gallon fresh apple cider
1 cup honey
½ cup orange juice
Juice of ½ lemon
6 to 7 cinnamon sticks
1 tablespoon whole cloves

½ teaspoon allspice
1 apple
1 orange
1 cup dark rum (optional)

Directions:

Add cider, honey, orange juice, lemon juice, cinnamon sticks, cloves, and allspice to a 2-gallon pot. Simmer on medium-low heat for 1 hour. Slice apple and orange into about six slices each, leaving the core and peels, and add to pot. Add rum. Serve warm.

BEVERAGES

Hot Maple Apple Cider

Courtesy of the Massachusetts Maple Producers Association

(www.massmaple.org)

Ingredients:

6 cups apple cider
¼ cup pure maple syrup
1 orange peel, cut into strips
1 lemon peel, cut into strips
2 cinnamon sticks

6 whole cloves
6 whole allspice berries
Spice bag
String

Directions:

Pour cider and syrup into large pot. Place peels and spices in center of a spice bag and tie with a piece of string. Drop spice bundle into liquid and heat over medium heat for about 10 minutes. Remove spice bag and discard. Ladle maple cider into mugs and serve warm.

Optional: Garnish with a stick of cinnamon for stirring, and top with whipped cream or a thin slice of lemon or orange.

Apple Toddy

Ingredients:

1 teaspoon white sugar
½ apple, baked
Water, as needed
Cider brandy (applejack), as needed
Grated nutmeg

Directions:

Dissolve 1 large teaspoonful of fine white sugar in a little boiling water. Pour into a hot bar-glass (middle-sized), and add 1 wineglassful of cider brandy (applejack) and half of a baked apple. Then fill the glass two-thirds full of boiling water, stir well, powder the top with grated nutmeg, and serve with a spoon.

Apple Ball Cocktail

Ingredients:
8 apples
Juice of 1 lemon
1 teaspoon salt
¼ pound (1 cup) white grapes
⅓ cup maraschino cherries
3 tablespoons syrup from cherries
Juice of ½ orange
Water

Directions:
Cut tops from stem end of the apples. Remove inside of apples with a French ball cutter, putting balls in 2 cups cold water with the lemon juice. Put the apple shells in 1 quart cold water to which is added 1 teaspoon salt. Remove skins and seeds from the white grapes. Just before serving drain apple shells. Remove apple balls from the water. Drain and mix with the white grapes and maraschino cherries and fill apple shells. Mix syrup from maraschino cherries with the orange juice and pour over the apple balls. Serve apple shells in individual dishes or cocktail glasses surrounded with crushed ice.

Note: Apple may be removed in small oval shapes with a coffee spoon, if a French ball cutter is not available.

Red Cooler

Ingredients:
2 cups cranberries
2 cups raspberries
1 cup 100% cran-raspberry juice
1 cup fat-free raspberry yogurt
2 cups ice

Directions:
Place all ingredients into blender and blend until smooth. Serve immediately.

Currant Julep

Ingredients:
1 tablespoon simple syrup (1 cup sugar, 2 cups water)
2 cups currants
2 cups water, cold
Fresh mint leaves
Raspberries, for garnish

Directions:
Begin by making the simple syrup by boiling 1 cup sugar and 2 cups water. Mash currants and cover with two cups of cold water. Strain and chill the juice. Put one tablespoon of the simple syrup in a tall glass, add three fresh mint leaves, and fill with the currant juice. Garnish with three or four raspberries and serve.

Magic Mint Hot Chocolate

Courtesy of Garelick Farms

(www.garelickfarms.com)

Ingredients:
2 cups Garelick Farms half & half
12 small dark chocolate covered peppermint patties
2 cups Garelick Farms 1% milk
Pinch of salt
Peppermint sticks, for garnish (optional)

Directions:
Combine 2/3 cup half and half with candy in heavy-bottomed saucepan. Stir continually with a wire whisk over low heat until patties melt. Stir in remaining half and half, milk, and salt and continue heating until mixture reaches simmering stage. Serve immediately. Garnish with peppermint sticks, if desired.

Fresh Mango Shake

Serves 1

Ingredients:

1 small mango (8 oz.) quartered, pitted, and peeled
¾ cup non-fat plain yogurt
⅓ cup orange juice
2 ice cubes

Directions:

Combine all the ingredients in a blender until thick and smooth.

Strawberry Yogurt Shake

Serves 2

Ingredients:

½ cup unsweetened pineapple juice
¾ cup plain low-fat yogurt
1½ cups frozen, unsweetened strawberries
1 teaspoon granulated sugar

Directions:

Add ingredients, in order listed, to blender container. Puree at medium speed, until thick and smooth.

Chocolate Milkshake

Ingredients:

2 tablespoons chopped ice
½ cup milk
2 tablespoons chocolate syrup
¼ cup seltzer (optional, for lighter shake)
3 tablespoons whipped cream

Directions:

Combine all ingredients together. Shake or stir well before drinking. A plainer drink can be made by combining the ice, ¾ cup milk, and syrup, then shaking well.

Note: A tablespoon of vanilla ice cream can also be added.

Maple Milkshake

Courtesy of the New York State Maple Producers Association

(www.nysmaple.com)

Ingredients:

2 scoops vanilla ice cream
1 cup milk
½ cup pure maple syrup

Directions:

Place ingredients in blender and blend until well mixed, or shake all ingredients thoroughly in a tightly covered container.

Berry Blast Smoothie

Ingredients:

2 cups blueberries
2 cups raspberries
2 cups strawberries
2 cups blackberries

1 cup 100% cran-raspberry juice
1 cup low-fat blueberry yogurt
2 cups ice

Directions:

Place all ingredients into blender and blend until smooth. Serve immediately.

Strawberry Kiwi Smoothie

Courtesy of the American Institute for Cancer Research

(www.aicr.org)

Ingredients:

1 cup 100% apple juice
1 (8 oz.) container strawberry fat-free yogurt

2 whole kiwi fruit, peeled and chopped
10 ounces unsweetened strawberries
1 teaspoon almond extract

Directions:

In blender, place apple juice, yogurt, and kiwi. Blend until smooth. Add strawberries and almond extract. Blend again until smooth and thick. Serve immediately.

Purifier Smoothie

Courtesy of Peter McClusky, Toronto Garlic Festival
(www.torontogarlicfestival.ca)
Serves 2

Ingredients:

1½ cups water (or coconut water or apple juice)
¾ cup kale, coarsely chopped
1 apple, cored and cut into quarters
¼ cup parsley, coarsely chopped
½ avocado, peeled and pit removed
1-2 garlic cloves, peeled

Directions:

Combine all ingredients in food processor and blend at medium speed for 30 seconds, or longer if a smoother consistency is desired. Serve in 8-ounce glasses.

Note: The parsley used in this recipe will help to eliminate garlic breath.

Kiddy Fruity Honey Smoothie

Courtesy of Benefits of Honey, the number one ranked website on the health benefits of honey
(www.benefits-of-honey.com)

Ingredients:

½ banana
5 strawberries
1 cup plain yogurt
2 teaspoons honey
Ice cubes

Directions:

Cut up the banana into pieces and put them into a blender with the strawberries. Add yogurt, honey, and ice cubes. Blend the mixture to make a delicious, smooth, cool drink.

"Revolutionary"

Sunflower

BREADS

Imagine eating your pasta without breadsticks or garlic bread, your eggs and bacon without toast, your beans without cornbread, or your pizza without the crust. It's just not the same, is it? Whether savory or sweet, bread makes a big difference in a lot of meals. In fact, there are some meals that simply aren't complete without it.

Bread is a staple food for many diets, and has been for centuries. In fact, history shows that there are types of breads that have been prepared for over 30,000 years. Although the main ingredients of bread are flour and water, a wide variety of other ingredients can also be tossed into the mix. Some types of breads contain yeast, milk, sugar, egg, cheese, spices, baking soda, vegetables, nuts, or seeds. Others, often termed "sweet breads," include tasty fresh or dried fruit or sweetening agents like pure maple syrup or honey.

Breads are not limited to one specific meal of the day. They can work with any meal and would accompany almost every type of meal. They fit easily into breakfast, lunch, dinner, or dessert. Many also work perfectly well on their own as a light snack or as a complement to an afternoon cup of coffee or tea, such as Cranberry and Almond Biscotti (page 157) or Old-Time Maple Gingerbread (page 155).

Cranberry Bread

Courtesy of Cape Cod Cranberry Growers' Association, Carver, MA

(www.cranberries.org)

Makes 1 loaf

Ingredients:

½ cup butter

1 cup sugar

1 tablespoon grated orange peel

1 teaspoon vanilla

3 large eggs, beaten

2½ cups flour

1 teaspoon baking soda

¼ teaspoon salt

¾ cup buttermilk

2 cups fresh cranberries, chopped

¾ cup pecans, chopped

Directions:

Preheat oven to 350°F. Spray bottom only of 9-inch x 5-inch loaf pan with cooking spray. Beat butter, sugar, orange peel, and vanilla in a large bowl until light and fluffy. Add eggs, mixing well. Combine flour, baking soda, and salt, then add to creamed mixture alternately with buttermilk, beating at low speed just until blended. Fold cranberries and nuts into batter. Turn into prepared pan, spreading evenly. Bake until wooden pick inserted in center comes out clean, about 50 to 60 minutes. Cool slightly in pan. Remove from pan and cool completely on wire rack.

Cranberry Swirl Bread

Courtesy of Cape Cod Cranberry Growers' Association, Carver, MA

(www.cranberries.org)

Ingredients:

Starter

1½ cups white whole-wheat flour

¾ cup cool water

Pinch instant yeast

Bread

All of the starter

2 cups white whole-wheat flour*

¼ cup all-purpose flour**

1 egg

¼ cup evaporated milk

3 tablespoons honey

½ teaspoon instant yeast

1 teaspoon salt

½ teaspoon lemon zest

¼ cup unsalted butter, softened

¾ cup dried sweetened cranberries

Filling

½ cup white sugar

2 teaspoon ground cinnamon

⅛ teaspoon ground cardamom (optional)

1 tablespoon all-purpose flour

1 egg

1 tablespoon water

Directions:

Starter

In a small bowl, combine the flour, water, and yeast together. Stir until smooth. Cover and let rest at room temperature overnight, or at least 6 hours.

Bread

Combine the starter, whole-wheat flour, all-purpose flour, egg, evaporated milk, honey, yeast, salt, and lemon zest in a mixing bowl. Mix on low to medium speed until the dough is smooth and pulls back when gently tugged on, about 5 minutes. Slowly add the softened butter while mixing on low speed until the dough is elastic and cleans the bowl. Add the cranberries in last and mix on low just until incorporated. Allow the dough to ferment for 1½ to 2 hours or until doubled.

Filling

Mix the sugar, spices, and flour together until well incorporated; set aside until needed. Combine the egg with the water in a separate bowl and refrigerate until needed.

To assemble the bread

Gently deflate the dough and roll out on a lightly floured surface to approximately 8 inches x 18 inches. Lightly egg wash the surface and sprinkle evenly with the sugar spice filling, leaving one of the short ends without filling to seal the bread roll. Beginning at the short end with filling, roll up towards the opposite end, but do not roll too tightly or too loosely. Once at the opposite end, seal the roll by pinching the unfilled end to the outer side of the roll; pinch the sides of the bread together to keep the filling from melting out during baking. Place the bread roll in a greased 9-inch x 5-inch bread pan and cover lightly with plastic wrap. Allow to proof for approximately 2 hours or until the dough crests over the top of the pan by about 1 inch. Bake in a pre-heated 375°F oven for about 30 to 35 minutes. The crust will be deep brown but not burned, and the internal temperature will register 195°F on a quick-read thermometer. Remove the bread from the pan immediately after removing from the oven and allow bread to cool on a cooling rack.

* Regular whole-wheat flour can be substituted for white whole-wheat flour.

** If using all-purpose flour in place of white whole-wheat flour, liquids may need adjusting.

Cranberry Oat Bread

Courtesy of the National Honey Board

(www.honey.com)

Makes 2 loaves

Ingredients:

¾ cup honey

⅓ cup vegetable oil

2 eggs

½ cup milk

2½ cups all-purpose flour

1 cup quick-cooking rolled oats

1 teaspoon baking soda

1 teaspoon baking powder

½ teaspoon salt

½ teaspoon ground cinnamon

2 cups fresh cranberries

1 cup chopped nuts

Directions:

Combine honey, oil, eggs, and milk in large bowl; mix well. Combine flour, oats, baking soda, baking powder, salt, and cinnamon in medium bowl; mix well. Stir into honey mixture. Fold in cranberries and nuts. Spoon into two 8½-inch x 4½-inch x 2½-inch greased and floured loaf pans. Bake in preheated 350°F oven 40 to 45 minutes or until wooden toothpick inserted near center comes out clean. Cool in pans on wire racks 15 minutes. Remove from pans; cool completely on wire racks.

Honey Apricot Bread

Courtesy of the American Beekeeping Federation (ABF)

(www.abfnet.org)

Ingredients:

3 cups flour

3 teaspoons baking powder

½ teaspoon salt

1 teaspoon cinnamon

¼ teaspoon nutmeg

1¼ cups milk

1 cup honey

1 egg, slightly beaten

2 tablespoons coconut oil or canola oil

1 cup chopped dried apricots, soaked in very hot water for 20-30 minutes

Directions:

In a large bowl, stir together flour, baking powder, salt, cinnamon, and nutmeg. In a separate bowl, combine milk, honey, eggs, and oil; pour over dry ingredients and stir just enough to dampen flour. Drain apricots and gently fold into batter. Pour into buttered loaf pan and bake in a 350°F oven for 60-70 minutes, or until done. Remove from pan. Serve with cream cheese spread.

Honey Whole-Wheat Bread

Courtesy of Janette Marshall from Health Benefits of Honey
(www.health-benefits-of-honey.com)

Ingredients:

7 cups whole-wheat flour (or 3 cups whole-wheat and 4 cups all-purpose flour)
2 packets quick-rise yeast
½ teaspoon salt
1⅔ cups very hot water (120°F-130°F)
½ cup honey
¼ cup vegetable oil
1 large egg
Poppy seeds, pumpkin seeds, crushed almonds or mixed nuts, to taste (optional)

Directions:

Preheat the oven to 350°F. In a large bowl, add together 3 cups of whole-wheat flour, yeast, and salt. Add hot water. Beat together the honey, oil, and egg and add this to your mixture along with one more cup of flour. Add the remaining flour slowly until the bread mixture no longer feels sticky. Punch and knead the dough for at least 10 minutes. Spread it out on a lightly floured surface, fold it, and push and punch it out again. The dough should feel smooth and elastic when you pull it. Cut the dough mixture into two equal halves, cover with plastic wrap, and let it sit for ten minutes. Take the two halves of dough and shape them into loaf shapes. Place them on a cookie sheet or flat baking tray, cover with a clean tea towel or more plastic wrap, and place in a warm room. Wait until the dough doubles in size (about 30 minutes). Use a sharp knife to cut an 'x' shape on top of each loaf and place them in the middle of the preheated oven. Once the bread is golden brown (approximately 20 minutes) place aluminum foil over the loaves and bake for another 10 minutes. The bread is done when a sharp knife is inserted and comes out clean. Take the bread out of the oven and, using a pastry brush, spread either honey or melted butter over the top to make it shine. Sprinkle any optional extras on top at this time. Place the loaves on a cooling rack and wait until they are still slightly warm before cutting.

Maple Oatmeal Bread

Courtesy of the New York State Maple Producers Association

(www.nysmaple.com)

Ingredients:

1 cup water, room temperature
½ cup regular rolled oats
1 tablespoon butter
2 tablespoons pure maple syrup
1 teaspoon salt

½ cup whole-wheat flour
2 cups bread flour
1½ tablespoons gluten
1½ teaspoons yeast

Directions:

Pour the room temperature water into a bowl. Add oats and let stand 20 minutes, if possible, before adding remaining ingredients in order listed. Bake in bread pan at 375°F for 28-30 minutes.

Variation: Use another tablespoon of maple syrup for more maple taste—the bread will also brown more.

Maple-Lemon Zucchini Bread

Courtesy of the New York State Maple Producers Association

(www.nysmaple.com)

Ingredients:

3 eggs
1 cup pure maple syrup
½ cup vegetable oil
1 teaspoon vanilla extract
Zest of 1 lemon, finely grated
1½ cups grated zucchini

1½ cups unbleached or all-purpose flour
1 cup whole whole-wheat
1 tablespoon baking powder
½ teaspoon salt

Directions:

Preheat oven to 350°F. Grease a 9- x 5-inch pan and set aside. Beat the eggs with an electric mixer for 2 minutes. Gradually add the maple syrup, oil, vanilla, and lemon zest. Stir in the zucchini. Combine the unbleached and wheat flours, baking powder, and salt in a large bowl. Make a well in the center, then stir in the zucchini mixture. Blend just until smooth, then turn into the prepared pan. Bake for 50 to 60 minutes, until a tester inserted into the center comes out clean. Cool in the pan for 5 to 10 minutes, then remove and cool completely on a wire rack.

Maple Monkey Bread

Courtesy of the New York State Maple Producers Association
(www.nysmaple.com)

Ingredients:

2 (7½ oz.) packs refrigerated biscuits
½ cup butter, melted
½ cup pure granulated maple sugar mixed with 1 teaspoon cinnamon
½ cup chopped walnuts (optional)
½ cup pure maple syrup

Directions:

Preheat oven to 350°F. Spray 10-inch bundt pan with non-stick cooking spray. Cut biscuits into quarters. Dip in melted butter, then roll the dough in the maple/cinnamon sugar and put in bundt pan in layers. Sprinkle chopped nuts as you go, if desired. Combine remaining butter and maple syrup and pour over top. Bake for 25-30 minutes or until golden brown. Be careful not to overcook or scorch. Immediately invert onto plate and pull pieces apart to serve.

Pumpkin Harvest Bread with Ice Cream

Ingredients:

1½ cups flour
½ cup cornmeal
1½ teaspoons baking powder
1 teaspoon baking soda
¼ teaspoon salt
2 teaspoons ground cinnamon
½ teaspoon ground nutmeg
1 cup solid pack cooked pumpkin

2 eggs
1 cup packed brown sugar
¼ cup vegetable oil
¼ cup apricot preserves
½ cup raisins
½ cup walnuts
4 cups low-fat vanilla ice cream

Directions:

Preheat the oven to 350°F. Combine the flour, cornmeal, baking powder, baking soda, salt, cinnamon, and nutmeg in a bowl. Beat the pumpkin, eggs, brown sugar, oil and preserves in a large mixing bowl. Incorporate the flour mixture and blend until well mixed. Stir in the raisins, walnuts, and transfer to a greased and floured loaf pan. Bake for 50 to 55 minutes or until wooden pick inserted into the center comes out clean. Cool in pan for 5 to 10 minutes. Transfer the loaf to a wire rack and cool completely before slicing. Serve each slice with ¼ cup low-fat vanilla ice cream.

Honey Pumpkin Tea Bread

Courtesy of the National Honey Board

(www.honey.com)

Makes 1 loaf

Ingredients:

½ cup (1 stick) unsalted butter, at room temperature, plus additional for the pan

2 cups all-purpose flour

1 teaspoon baking soda

½ teaspoon salt

½ teaspoon ground cinnamon

½ teaspoon ginger

½ teaspoon grated nutmeg

1 cup honey

1 cup fresh pumpkin puree

2 eggs, room temperature

2 teaspoons lemon juice

1 teaspoon vanilla extract

Directions:

Preheat oven to 350°F. Position rack in center of oven. Generously butter a 9-inch x 5-inch metal loaf pan and set aside. Sift flour, baking soda, salt, cinnamon, ginger and nutmeg into a medium bowl. Set aside. In a large bowl, combine butter and honey and beat with an electric mixer at medium speed for 2 minutes or until smooth. Add the pumpkin; beat for 1 minute or until well combined. Beat in eggs one at a time, beating each for 1 minute. Stir in lemon juice and vanilla extract. Add the sifted dry ingredients. With the mixer on low, beat just until incorporated. Increase mixer speed to medium and beat for 2 minutes or until the batter is smooth, scraping down the sides of the bowl as necessary with a rubber spatula. Spread into prepared pan. Bake about 65 minutes, or until a cake tester or wooden skewer inserted into the middle of the loaf comes out clean. Cool the bread on a wire rack for 10 minutes, slide out of mold, and continue cooling on the rack for 30 minutes before cutting.

HEALTH BENEFITS OF PUMPKINS

Pumpkins are packed full of beneficial vitamins, minerals, and nutrients. They are high in vitamins A, C, K, and E. They contain high levels of alpha and beta-carotene, antioxidant carotenoids, fiber, water, and essential minerals like zinc, iron, magnesium, and potassium. The fruit of the pumpkin also serves as a natural laxative. The seeds, oil, and juice from pumpkins have many health and nutritional properties as well.

Pumpkin Bread

Contributed by Chef Nancy Berkoff, The Vegetarian Resource Group, Vegetarian Journal
(www.vrg.org)
Makes two 8-inch loaves or 24 muffins

Ingredients:

3 cups unbleached flour
½ teaspoon baking powder
1 teaspoon baking soda
1 teaspoon cinnamon
1 teaspoon nutmeg
1 teaspoon cloves
1 teaspoon ginger
2 cups sugar (use your favorite vegan variety)
1 cup brown sugar (use your favorite vegan variety)

¾ cup oil or mashed bananas
½ cup soft tofu
2 cups canned pumpkin (not sweetened or spiced) or 2 cups stewed and pureed fresh pumpkin
1 cup raisins
½ cup chopped walnuts (optional)
Vegetable oil spray

Directions:

Preheat oven to 350°F. Spray two small loaf pans or place insert paper into 24 muffin cups. Sift together flour, baking powder, baking soda, and spices. In a mixer bowl, mix together sugars, oil or bananas, and tofu. Add pumpkin and mix well. Mixing on slow speed, gradually add flour and mix until well combined. Add in raisins and nuts. Pour into prepared pans. Bake for 45 minutes or until a knife inserted in the center comes out clean. Allow to coo

Note: Pumpkin has lots of fiber and nutrients and adds a pleasant texture to many foods.

This pumpkin bread is just sweet enough to serve toasted for breakfast or for dessert, yet it is savory enough to serve at lunch or dinner.

Cornbread

Courtesy of Debra Wasserman and Reed Mangels, Ph.D., R.D., "Simply Vegan", The
Vegetarian Resource Group
(www.vrg.org)

Ingredients:

1 cup cornmeal
1 cup whole-wheat flour
1 tablespoon baking powder

¼ cup oil
1 cup soy milk
⅓ cup molasses or pure maple syrup

Directions:

Preheat oven to 375°F. Mix ingredients together in bowl. Pour batter into lightly oiled 8-inch round pan. Bake for 20 minutes.

Variation: Prepare same batter, and pour into lightly oiled muffin tins. Bake at the same temperature for the same amount of time. Children will especially enjoy these muffins.

Pumpkin Indian Cakes

Ingredients:
Stewed pumpkin
Corn meal
Butter

Directions:
Mash the stewed pumpkin, drain thoroughly in a sieve or colander, and place into a pan. Using an equal portion of corn meal, gradually stir the meal into the stewed pumpkin, adding a little butter as you stir. Mix thoroughly, stirring it very hard. If the mixture is not thick enough to form a stiff dough, add a little more corn meal. Form the mixture into round, flat cakes (about the size of a muffin), and bake them on a hot griddle greased with butter. As an alternative, you can lay them in a square iron pan and bake them in an oven. Serve hot with butter.

Apple Loaf

Ingredients:
2 cups flour
2 teaspoons baking powder
1 teaspoon salt
1 cup sugar
1 tablespoon shortening

1 egg
Milk, as needed
Apples, as needed

Directions:
Mix together flour, baking powder, salt, sugar, and shortening. Break the egg into the flour mixture. Add sufficient milk to make a stiff batter, and pour into a shallow pan. Pare and slice apples, covering the top of the batter. Bake at 350°F for 50-60 minutes, or until inserted toothpick comes out clean. When almost done, sprinkle sugar over the apples.

Old-Time Maple Gingerbread

Courtesy of the Massachusetts Maple Producers Association

(www.massmaple.org)

Ingredients:

2 cups flour

1 teaspoon ginger

½ teaspoon salt

1 teaspoon baking soda

1 cup pure maple syrup

1 egg, beaten

1 cup sour cream

Directions:

Combine and sift dry ingredients. Mix maple syrup with beaten egg and add the sour cream. Combine the mixture and bake in medium oven for about 40 minutes. Serve with warm maple hard sauce or whipped cream.

Currant Sweet Biscuits

Ingredients:

¾ cup flour

1 teaspoon salt

½ cup sugar

3 tablespoons baking powder

4 tablespoons shortening

1 egg

1 cup milk

1 cup currants, washed

Directions:

Sift all dry ingredients together, except for currants. Beat in shortening, egg, and milk. Add the currants and work dough in the bowl until smooth. Turn the dough onto a lightly floured board and cut the biscuits. Lightly brush the tops with milk and bake at 425°F for about 15 minutes.

Maple Biscuits

Courtesy of Shaver-Hill Farm

(www.shaverhillfarm.com)

Ingredients:

2 cups all-purpose flour

¾ teaspoon salt

1 tablespoon baking powder

4 tablespoons cold butter

¾ cup heavy cream

¼ cup pure maple syrup

2 tablespoons butter, melted

2 tablespoons pure maple syrup

Directions:

Preheat oven to 425°F. Combine dry ingredients in mixing bowl. Cut the butter into the flour mixture until it resembles coarse meal. Blend the heavy cream and ¼ cup maple syrup and pour into a well in the flour mixture. Stir until a sticky dough forms. Turn the dough onto a lightly floured surface and gently knead four or five times. Pat or roll to a ¾-inch thickness. Cut into rounds with a biscuit cutter or glass and place on lightly greased baking sheet. Melt 2 tablespoons of butter and mix with 2 tablespoons of maple syrup, stirring to blend. Brush some of the maple syrup and butter mixture on each biscuit. Bake until golden, about 15 minutes. Serve hot.

Currant Buns

Ingredients:

2 large potatoes

⅔ cake of yeast or 2 (¼ oz.) packages or 4½ teaspoons dry yeast

1 cup sugar

1 tablespoon butter

1 teaspoon salt

3 cups flour

1–1½ cups currants

Directions:

Boil the potatoes and strain the water into a pitcher. Dissolve two-thirds cake of yeast in a cup. Put potatoes in a pan with sugar, butter, and salt. Mash them until creamy. Pour in the rest of potato water, 2 cups flour, and yeast, then mix together. Cover and set in a warm place for the night. The next morning, add the currants and remaining cup of flour while you turn the dough quickly. This will keep them from settling in the bottom of the bread. Put in hot pans and bake in a hot oven. Serve hot or cold.

Cranberry and Almond Biscotti

Courtesy of the American Institute for Cancer Research

(www.aicr.org)

Ingredients:

¾ cup dried cranberries

¾ cup whole almonds

1 cup sugar, divided

1¼ cups unbleached all-purpose flour

¾ cup whole-wheat pastry flour

½ teaspoon baking powder

½ teaspoon baking soda

1 teaspoon ground cinnamon

¼ teaspoon salt

¼ cup golden raisins

3 eggs, lightly beaten

1 teaspoon vanilla extract

⅛ teaspoon almond extract

Directions:

Cover cranberries in warm water in a small bowl and soak to plump them, about 20 minutes. Drain, gently squeeze out excess moisture and pat them dry with a paper towel. Set a rack in the center of the oven, and preheat to 350°F. Line a baking sheet with parchment paper (or foil lightly coated with canola oil spray). Set aside. Grind the almonds with 2 tablespoons of the sugar, pulsing in 5-second bursts until most of the almonds are a powder, about 30 seconds. Place the nuts in a large mixing bowl. Add the remaining sugar, both flours, baking powder, baking soda, cinnamon, and salt to the nuts. Toss the cranberries and raisins with a tablespoon of this mixture, then stir them into the dry ingredients, mixing well. Mix in the eggs, vanilla, almond extract and 2 tablespoons water. With a wooden spoon, mix until a sticky, dense dough forms, working in all the flour. Halve the dough. Moistening your hands lightly with cold water, shape the dough into two flattened 13-inch x 2½-inch logs, spaced 4 inches apart on the lined baking sheet. Bake until golden and firm to the touch, about 25 minutes. Cool logs on the baking sheet for 15 minutes. Transfer logs to a cutting board. With a serrated knife, cut each log diagonally into ½-inch thick slices. Arrange them cut-side down in one layer on the baking sheet, with slices touching each other. Bake 10 minutes, turn, and bake 10 more minutes, or until biscotti are a honey color and dry to the touch. Turn the oven off and leave biscotti there for 10 more minutes. Remove them from the oven and let them cool on the baking sheet. Store sealed in an air-tight container for up to 3 weeks.

Note: For a sophisticated but healthful treat, try these whole-wheat biscotti with almonds and fruit.

SAUCES, DIPS & PRESERVES

Although sauces, dips, dressings, and preserves fall into a category that generally doesn't stand on its own, they still have an important function in appetizers, entrées, side dishes, breakfasts, salads, and desserts. They help add the finishing touches to a variety of delicious foods.

Can you picture how bland your biscuit would taste without the sweet punch of flavor from your homemade Strawberry Jelly (page 177) or Fruit and Nuts Honey Butter (page 172)? Imagine serving your party guests a heaping platter of raw vegetables fresh from the garden, but forgetting to set out the dips, dressings, and hummus. How about munching on a bowl of tortilla chips without dipping them in salsa or cheese sauce or eating a green salad without any dressing? All of the above items can be eaten without the addition of sauces, dips, and spreads, and the foods would still be edible, but the result of the all-important taste test would simply not be the same. While dips, preserves, and sauces don't comprise the meal or dish on their own, they often complete it.

Surprise your family with a delicious topping of Spicy Apple and Pear Chutney (page 163) the next time you prepare grilled fish, pork, or poultry. Tickle your guests' taste buds at your next get-together with an assortment of toasted pita bread and fresh vegetables from your local farmers market, served with a savory Feta Cheese Spread (page 168) or Cucumber Yogurt Dip (page 166).

Honey Mustard Dressing

Courtesy of Janette Marshall from Health Benefits of Honey
(www.health-benefits-of-honey.com)

Ingredients:

½ cup olive oil
2 teaspoons Dijon mustard
⅛ cup balsamic vinegar
2 teaspoons red wine vinegar
¼ cup grated ginger

Juice and zest of 1 lemon
2 teaspoons coriander
6 small carrots, grated
2 teaspoons honey (preferable raw honey)

Directions:

Mix the olive oil, mustard, balsamic vinegar, red wine vinegar, ginger, lemon juice and zest, and coriander in a saucepan. Gently cook the mixture on low heat, stirring often. Add the grated carrots. The honey mustard sauce will thicken after about 30 minutes. Add the honey at the end (excessive heat will destroy honey's health benefits). Serve this honey mustard dressing with cold or grilled meats. It works well with honey baked ham and white fish dishes.

Maple Blender French Dressing

Courtesy of the New York State Maple Producers Association
(www.nysmaple.com)
Makes 2 cups

Ingredients:

1 cup ketchup
½ cup pure maple syrup
1 teaspoon salt
¾ cup salad oil (such as safflower, olive, canola, or sunflower)

¼ teaspoon pepper
½ teaspoon dry mustard
½ teaspoon powdered ginger

Directions:

Place all ingredients in blender, cover, and blend on high speed for 20 seconds.

Maple Vinaigrette Salad Dressing

Courtesy of the New York State Maple Producers Association

(www.nysmaple.com)

Ingredients:

½ cup pure granulated maple sugar
½ cup white vinegar
½ cup canola oil
½ teaspoon paprika
¼ teaspoon garlic powder

½ teaspoon dry mustard
¼ teaspoon pepper
½ teaspoon Mrs. Dash® Table Blend Seasoning
½ teaspoon Worcestershire sauce

Directions:

Combine all ingredients in a bottle that will seal tightly. Shake vigorously prior to use. Store in refrigerator.

Note: This salad dressing is almost entirely salt-free! There is a negligible amount of salt in the Worcestershire sauce.

Ketchup

Makes 3 pints

Ingredients:

4 quarts tomatoes, cored, peeled, and chopped
1 cup onion, chopped
¼ cup red pepper
1½ teaspoons celery seed
1 teaspoon whole allspice
1 teaspoon mustard seed

1 cinnamon stick
1 cup sugar
1 tablespoon salt
1 tablespoon paprika
1½ cups distilled white vinegar

Directions:

Prepare jars, lids, and hot water bath canner according to manufacturer instructions.

Combine tomatoes, onions, and peppers in a large stainless steel saucepan. Cook over medium heat until soft. Strain through a food mill. Return hot mixture to large stainless steel saucepan and cook over medium-high heat, stirring frequently for about 1 hour or until the mixture is reduced by half. Tie spices in a spice bag and add spice bag, sugar, salt, and paprika to the hot mixture. Cook over low heat, stirring often, for 25 minutes. Add vinegar and continue cooking until the mixture is the consistency of thick ketchup. Remove spice bag.

Using a ladle and a funnel, spoon the hot mixture into prepared, hot sterile jars. Leave ¼ inch head space and remove air bubbles. Wipe the outer rim of the jars with a clean damp cloth to ensure a tight fit. Adjust the two-piece lids and secure snugly.

Place jars in hot water bath canner, making sure the water covers the jars by at least 1 inch. Boil for 10 minutes. Turn heat off, remove jars, and cool overnight. Remove outer lid and store.

SAUCES, DIPS & PRESERVES

Pink Lady Apple Salsa

Ingredients:

1 large tomato, cored and finely chopped
¾ cup finely chopped sweet onion
3 tablespoons freshly squeezed lime juice
1 large jalapeño chile, cored, seeded and finely chopped
2 Pink Lady apples
2 tablespoons minced fresh cilantro

1 tablespoon honey
Salt and freshly ground black pepper, to taste
Corn chips

Directions:

Stir together the tomato, onion, lime juice, and jalapeño in a medium bowl. Quarter and core the Pink Lady apples and cut them into fine dice. Stir the apples into the tomato mixture with the cilantro, honey and salt and pepper to taste. Refrigerate for up to 6 hours before serving. To serve, spoon the salsa into a serving bowl and serve with a bowl of corn chips alongside.

Note: Delicious as an appetizer served with corn chips, this salsa could also be spooned over a piece of grilled or baked halibut or other fish.

Spicy Mango Currant Salsa

Ingredients:

3 mangos, diced small
½ cup pineapple, diced small
¼ medium-sized red onion, diced small
½ cup currants
¼ cup cilantro, finely chopped
3 tablespoons olive oil
½ teaspoon garam masala, or to taste

1 large clove garlic, minced
2 ounces controlled moisture red pepper (about ½ pepper), diced small
1 fire-roasted and seeded habañero chili, diced small
2 limes, juiced
⅓ teaspoon salt, kosher

Directions:

Toss all ingredients together in a bowl, cover, and allow it to marinate for one hour. Taste and adjust seasoning if needed.

Suggested Serving: Serve over grilled light fish such as halibut, cod, or bass.

Cranberry Salsa

Ingredients:

4 ounces 100% cranberry juice blend
1½ cups diced tomatoes
1 cup fresh cranberries, sliced thin
¼ cup ripe medium avocado, diced
½ cup diced pineapple
½ cup thinly sliced scallions (including green tops)

2 tablespoons lemon juice
¼ cup finely chopped jalapeño peppers
2 cloves crushed garlic (about 1 teaspoon)
Fresh ground pepper, to taste

Directions:

Place juice into a saucepan. Boil for about 5 minutes until reduced to about 1 tablespoon of syrup. Place the reduced juice and all remaining ingredients into a medium bowl and stir until incorporated. Chill and serve immediately with favorite chips and vegetables.

Note: Fresh cranberries may be stored in your freezer for up to 1 year.

Spicy Apple and Pear Chutney

Ingredients:

1¾ cup finely diced Gala apples
1¾ cup finely diced Bartlett pears
2 tablespoons lemon juice
2 tablespoons chopped cilantro
1 clove garlic, finely chopped

½ cup finely chopped red onion
1½ teaspoons sugar
¼ teaspoon salt
¼ teaspoon red pepper flakes

Directions:

Combine all ingredients. Chill at least 2 hours.

Note: This chutney is a great accompaniment to grilled fish, pork or poultry.

SAUCES, DIPS & PRESERVES

Gooseberry Chutney

Ingredients:

2 pints gooseberries, nearly ripe
¾ pound raisins
3 onions, diced
1 cup brown sugar
3 tablespoons mustard
3 tablespoons ginger
3 tablespoons salt

¼ teaspoon red pepper
Pinch turmeric
2 pints vinegar

Directions:

Mix gooseberries, raisins, and onions. Chop together and heat slowly with brown sugar and all seasonings. Simmer for 40 minutes with vinegar, then strain through coarse sieve. Seal in small jars.

Chunky Cranberry Dip

Courtesy of the American Institute for Cancer Research
(www.aicr.org)
Makes about 1½ cups

Ingredients:

1 (8 oz.) package reduced fat cream cheese
1-2 tablespoons low-fat milk
½ cup chopped dried cranberries
¼ cup chopped blanched almonds
½ teaspoon orange zest, preferably fresh

Directions:

In medium bowl, place cream cheese and allow to soften at room temperature. Mash and work with fork until texture is light enough to combine easily with other ingredients. Gradually add milk until cream cheese becomes soft and spreadable. Mix in remaining ingredients. Cover and refrigerate up to 2 days ahead or let stand at room temperature 1 hour before serving to allow flavors to blend.

Note: Good for spreading on half a whole-wheat bagel.

Chickpea Dip

Serves 4

Ingredients:

3 cloves garlic
¼ cup plain low-fat yogurt
1 tablespoon fresh lemon juice
1 teaspoon olive oil
¼ teaspoon salt

¼ teaspoon paprika
⅛ teaspoon pepper
1 (19 oz.) can chickpeas, drained

Directions:

Put all ingredients into a food processor and blend until smooth. Serve at room temperature with pita chips, crackers, carrots, or other dipping vegetables.

Artichokes with Garlic Dip

Serves 4

Ingredients:

1 cup plain low-fat yogurt
1 tablespoon chopped parsley
1 tablespoon chopped chives
2 teaspoons chili sauce
2 cloves garlic, minced
⅛ teaspoon pepper
4 artichokes (medium), prepared and cooked

Directions:

Combine all ingredients (except artichokes); blend well. Refrigerate until serving. Serve with cooked artichokes.

SAUCES, DIPS & PRESERVES

Cucumber Yogurt Dip

Serves 6

Ingredients:

2 large cucumbers, peeled, seeded, and grated

2 cups plain low-fat yogurt

½ cup non-fat sour cream

1 tablespoon lemon juice

1 tablespoon fresh dill

1 garlic clove, chopped

1 cup cherry tomatoes

1 cup broccoli florets

1 cup baby carrots

Directions:

Peel, seed, and grate one cucumber. Slice the other cucumber and set aside. Mix yogurt, grated cucumber, sour cream, lemon juice, dill, and garlic in a serving bowl. Chill for 1 hour. Arrange tomatoes, sliced cucumbers, broccoli, and carrots on a colorful platter. Serve with cucumber dip.

Savory Dip

Courtesy of Benefits of Honey, the number one ranked website
on the health benefits of honey
(www.benefits-of-honey.com)

Ingredients:

½ cup tomato sauce

1 teaspoon cornstarch

½ teaspoon garlic salt

¼ cup honey

2 tablespoons lemon juice

Directions:

Combine all ingredients and cook in a saucepan for a few minutes. Allow mixture to boil and thicken while stirring it to smooth the mixture. This serves as a delicious dip for sizzling hot barbecue wings or chicken nuggets.

Cheese Fondue

Ingredients:

2 pounds mild American cheese
2 quarts scalded milk
2 quarts soft, stale bread crumbs
½ cup butter

4 teaspoons mustard
4 teaspoons salt
1 teaspoon paprika
24 eggs, yolks separated

Directions:

Grate or chop cheese. Mix remaining ingredients (except eggs) together, add well-beaten yolks, then cut and fold in stiffly beaten whites. Pour into six buttered baking dishes and bake for thirty minutes on medium heat.

Warm Roasted Tomato Bruschetta

Courtesy of the Central New York Tomatofest, from the kitchen of Nadine Vande Walker
(www.cnytomatofest.org)

Ingredients:

Topping

4–5 medium fresh tomatoes, diced
¾ cup diced red and green peppers
¾ cup diced onions
2 cloves sliced garlic
2 tablespoons extra-virgin olive oil
2 teaspoons kosher salt
1 teaspoon fresh ground pepper
1 teaspoon sugar

¼ teaspoon crushed red pepper flakes
2 tablespoons fresh sliced basil, divided
1 tablespoon freshly grated Parmesan cheese

Toasted Bread

1 fresh baguette loaf
½ cup garlic butter (purchase or make your own)

Directions:

Topping

Preheat oven to 425°F. Spread out the first four ingredients on a cookie sheet or stoneware bar pan. Drizzle with the olive oil and add salt, pepper, sugar, red pepper, and 1 tablespoon of basil. Roast the tomatoes and vegetables for 30 to 40 minutes until the tomatoes, peppers, and onions are tender and a little brown around the edges and all liquid has evaporated (the consistency should be a little thick). Place the tomato mixture in a bowl and top with remaining fresh basil and freshly grated Parmesan cheese. Place bowl onto a serving plate with toasted bread.

Toasted Bread

Slice baguette in half and spread garlic butter on both sides of the bread. Place bread under broiler for 3–5 minutes, until butter is melted and bread is slightly browned around the edges. Slice and serve with warm tomato mixture.

SAUCES, DIPS & PRESERVES

Maple Cream Cheese Spread

Courtesy of the New York State Maple Producers Association

(www.nysmaple.com)

Ingredients:

½ cup pure maple cream
6 ounces cream cheese, softened

Directions:

In a food processor or with an electric mixer, whip the maple cream and the cream cheese together until light and fluffy. The spread can be refrigerated in a covered container for up to 3 weeks.

Feta Cheese Spread

Courtesy of Mt. Vikos®

(www.mtvikos.com)

Ingredients:

6 ounces Mt. Vikos® barrel-aged feta cheese, crumbled
4 ounces cream cheese, room temperature
4 ounces sour cream
3 teaspoons lemon juice, freshly squeezed
1 teaspon granulated garlic or garlic powder
3 teaspoons fresh dill, finely chopped
¼ teaspoon cayenne

Directions:

With a large fork, blend all ingredients in a mixing bowl until the mixture is smooth. Refrigerate for one hour. Garnish with fresh dill. Serve with fresh vegetables or toasted pita

10-Minute Cranberry Sauce

Ingredients:

2 cups sugar
2 cups water
4 cups cranberries

Directions:

Boil sugar and water together for five minutes. Add cranberries and boil, without stirring, until all the skins pop open, about five minutes. Remove from heat. Pour into a mold and allow to cool before serving.

Roasted Garlic Spread with Sweet or Savory Toppings

Courtesy of Peter McClusky, Toronto Garlic Festival

(www.torontogarlicfestival.ca)

Makes 6 appetizers

Ingredients:

20 garlic cloves, skin left on
2 tablespoons olive oil
½ teaspoon kosher salt
1 teaspoon freshly ground black pepper

Puree

1 tablespoon olive oil
1 teaspoon thyme
Kosher salt and freshly ground black pepper, to taste

Directions:

Pre-heat oven to 325°F. Place garlic cloves on baking sheet or casserole dish and drizzle with oil, salt, and pepper. Gently stir ingredients so that the oil coats each clove. Cover with aluminum foil or a lid and bake at 325°F for 30 minutes to one hour (depending on the size of the garlic cloves). To check for doneness, a fork should easily pierce the garlic. Remove from oven and allow to cool for ten minutes. To remove the flesh from the cloves, hold each clove and press gently, squeezing the flesh through the sprouting end of the clove. Some parts of the clove may be a deep golden brown, due to caramelization of the sugars in the clove during cooking. Take care to include this part.

Puree

Place roasted garlic, olive oil, and thyme in a food processor and mix for 30 seconds or until desired consistency is achieved. Alternatively, a potato masher can be used instead of a processor. Add salt and pepper to taste. Serve on crackers or toasted baguette slices. This spread can also be accompanied with an assortment of savory toppings such as goat cheese, mozzarella, or gruyère cheese, along with thinly sliced roasted bell pepper, sun-dried tomatoes, olives, or capers. Suggested sweet toppings include pure peach marmalade, mango chutney, or brandied plum jam.

Note: This roasted garlic spread can also be used as a base in soup (such as Flu Fighter Garlic Soup on page 33), in sandwiches (such as Roasted Garlic Grilled Cheese Sandwich on page 104), or as a condiment on a baked potato.

SAUCES, DIPS & PRESERVES

Sweet Spiced Blackberry Sauce

Ingredients:
1 cup blackberries, washed
1 cup sugar
1¼ cups water
½ teaspoon nutmeg
1 teaspoon cinnamon
½ teaspoon allspice
3 tablespoons cornstarch

Directions:
Place blackberries, sugar, and 1 cup of water in a saucepan. Blend spices and add to berry mixture. Cook slowly over medium heat until the fruit is soft. Rub through a fine sieve and thicken with the cornstarch dissolved in ¼ cup water. Bring sauce to a boil and cook for 5 minutes. Cool and serve.

Garlic Butter and Garlic in Olive Oil

Courtesy of Hood River Garlic Farm
(www.hoodrivergarlic.com)

Ingredients:

Butter
1½ cups butter
1 cup crushed garlic (or more, up to ½ cup)

Olive Oil
½ cup extra-virgin olive oil
⅓ cup crushed garlic (or more, to taste)

Directions:

Butter

Mash garlic cloves in mini chopper and mix into soft butter. Add chives, parsley and salt if desired. Form into logs, wrap in waxed paper, and place in freezer bags or plastic wrap. Store in freezer and slice as needed.

Olive Oil

Crush the garlic as you would with the garlic butter. Then evenly distribute the crushed garlic into the bottom of a zip lock bag. Add enough olive oil to completely cover all the crushed garlic and blend gently by rubbing the outside of the bag. Freeze and slice as needed.

Pumpkin Butter

Ingredients:
2 pounds or pints dry mashed pumpkin
1 pound sugar
4 ounces butter
Flavoring either of shaved lemon rind, cloves, nutmeg or ginger (not pulverized)

Directions:
Bake or steam the pumpkin, then mash it through a strainer. Mix together the pumpkin, sugar, butter, and flavoring (lemon rind, cloves, nutmeg, or ginger). Let the mixture simmer on the stove for about an hour until it becomes thick and semitransparent.

Apple Butter
Makes 5-6 pints

Ingredients:
2 quarts apple cider
4 quarts apples
2 cups sugar

2 cups dark corn syrup
1 teaspoon cinnamon

Directions:
Boil the cider until reduced to 1 quart. Pare the apples and slice thin. Put the apples into the cider and cook very slowly, stirring frequently, until it begins to thicken. Add sugar, syrup, and cinnamon then continue to cook until thick enough to spread when cool. Seal in sterilized jars.

Cinnamon Flavor Honey Butter
Courtesy of Benefits of Honey, the number one ranked website
on the health benefits of honey (www.benefits-of-honey.com)
Serves 10

Ingredients:
¼ cup soft butter or margarine
¼ teaspoon cinnamon powder
½ cup creamed honey
1 tablespoon cream cheese (optional)

Directions:
Blend all ingredients in a bowl and beat well until mixture is smooth and creamy. Spread the honey butter on piping hot toasted bread or biscuits.

SAUCES, DIPS & PRESERVES

Easy Maple Butter

Courtesy of the New York State Maple Producers Association

(www.nysmaple.com)

Ingredients:

½ cup butter, softened

¼ cup pure maple syrup

Directions:

In a food processor, whip butter until creamy. Gradually add the maple syrup and whip until the mixture is smooth.

Note: This maple butter is delicious served on waffles or spread on thin, rolled crepes.

Fruit and Nuts Honey Butter

Courtesy of Benefits of Honey, the number one ranked website

on the health benefits of honey

(www.benefits-of-honey.com)

Ingredients:

¼ cup soft butter or margarine

1 tablespoon peanuts or walnuts

1 tablespoon finely cut dried tropical fruits

½ cup creamed honey

Directions:

Stir and blend all ingredients in a bowl. Mix well. Spread honey butter on soft bread or biscuits.

"Eating is an agricultural act."

—Wendell Berry

Concord Grape Jam
Makes 6 half-pint jars

Ingredients:
8 cups Concord grapes (stemmed)
6 cups sugar

Directions:
Prepare jars, lids, and hot water bath canner according to manufacturer instructions.

Separate grape skins with fingers by squeezing out the grape pulp and placing in a pot. Place skins in a separate pot. Bring pulp to a boil, stirring frequently, over medium heat for about 10 minutes or until pulp is soft. Strain pulp through a sieve to remove the seeds. Let stand.

To prevent burning, add a small amount of water to the pot containing the skins. Bring to a boil over medium heat and then lower the heat. Boil the skins gently until they are soft and the liquid is nearly evaporated (about 10 minutes).

Combine skins, pulp, and sugar in a large deep stainless steel saucepan. Bring to a boil over medium heat, stirring constantly to dissolve the sugar. Continue to boil mixture, stirring frequently, until the mixture has thickened and is at the gel stage (20–30 minutes, depending upon the fruit used). To test for the gel stage, dip a spoon into the hot fruit mixture and place the mixture on a chilled saucer. Place the saucer in the freezer for 1 minute. Push one finger through the spread. If the mixture is at the gel stage, it will be set and the surface will crinkle when pushing a finger through.

When gel stage has been reached, remove the hot mixture from the stove and skim off any foam.

Using a ladle and a funnel, spoon the hot jam mixture into prepared, sterile jars. Leave ¼ inch head space and remove air bubbles. Wipe the outer rim of the jars with a clean damp cloth to ensure a tight fit. Adjust the two-piece lids and secure snugly.

Place jars in hot water bath canner, making sure the water covers the jars by at least 1 inch. Boil for 10 minutes. Turn heat off, remove jars, and cool overnight. Remove outer lid and store.

Note: This recipe does not use pectin because the fruit naturally contains enough pectin. Because pectin is not being added, be sure to use ⅓ under-ripened fruit and ⅔ fully ripened fruit.

SAUCES, DIPS & PRESERVES

Peach Jam

Makes 7 half-pint jars

Ingredients:

8 cups ripe soft peaches, chopped, pitted, and peeled
4 tablespoons lemon juice (preferably freshly squeezed)
6 cups sugar

Directions:

Prepare jars, lids, and hot water bath canner according to manufacturer instructions.

Blanch peaches in boiling water for 30–60 seconds to remove skins. Combine peaches, lemon juice, and sugar in a deep stainless steel saucepan. Bring to a boil over medium heat, stirring constantly. Boil, stirring frequently, until the mixture has thickened and is at the gel stage (20–30 minutes, depending upon the fruit used). To test for the gel stage, dip a spoon into the hot fruit mixture and place the mixture on a chilled saucer. Place the saucer in the freezer for 1 minute. Push one finger through the spread. If the mixture is at the gel stage, it will be set and the surface will crinkle when pushing a finger through.

When gel stage has been reached, remove the hot mixture from the stove and skim off any foam.

Using a ladle and a funnel, spoon the hot jam mixture into prepared, sterile jars. Leave ¼ inch head space and remove air bubbles. Wipe the outer rim of the jars with a clean damp cloth to ensure a tight fit. Adjust the two-piece lids and secure snugly.

Place jars in hot water bath canner, making sure the water covers the jars by at least 1 inch. Boil for 10 minutes. Turn heat off, remove jars, and cool overnight. Remove outer lid and store.

Note: This recipe does not use pectin because the fruit naturally contains enough pectin. Because pectin is not being added, be sure to use ⅓ under-ripened fruit and ⅔ fully ripened fruit.

Maple Jelly

Courtesy of the Massachusetts Maple Producers Association
(www.massmaple.org)

Ingredients:

3 cups cold water
2 teaspoons Genugel® (pectin does not work with maple syrup)
½ gallon Grade A Medium Amber pure maple syrup

Directions:

Whisk the Genugel® into the cold water first, then add to syrup. Make sure the pot is at least three times the size of the liquid, as it foams up during boil. Boil all ingredients to 217.5°F. Some people prefer to boil to 219°F, but that makes unnecessarily hard jelly and wastes more content. The objective is to make clear jelly. Any infusion of air through stirring or filling of the jars will put air bubbles into the jelly. It will still taste fine, but won't look as appealing. It helps greatly to keep a low flame under the jelly while bottling, as it will gel really fast and heat keeps it liquid longer. First, skim off the surface foam as minimally as possible to prevent waste. Then use a cup or ladle large enough to fill each clean jar with one pour. Going back and adding more to fill the jar will cause air bubbles and layering. Cap the filled jars and process them in a hot water bath for 10 minutes at 180°F. Depending on how successful you are at skimming, a half gallon of syrup will net you five to seven 8-oz. jars of maple jelly.

Note: Genugel® is available from maple syrup equipment suppliers.

MAKING MAPLE SYRUP

- It takes 40 to 50 gallons of sap to make 1 gallon of maple syrup.
- Maple syrup is 100% fat free!
- The season for tapping trees only lasts for 8-10 weeks and runs from February until early April.

SAUCES, DIPS & PRESERVES

Blueberry Jelly

Makes 5 half-pint jars

Ingredients:

3½ cups natural unsweetened blueberry juice (see note below)
2 tablespoons lemon juice
1 (1¾ oz.) package powdered pectin
5 cups sugar

Directions:

Prepare jars, lids, and hot water bath canner according to manufacturer instructions.

Place blueberry juice and lemon juice in a large stainless steel saucepan and whisk in powdered pectin until dissolved. Bring mixture to a boil over high heat, stirring constantly. Add sugar and return mixture to a full rolling boil, stirring constantly. Continue the rolling boil for 1 minute. Remove from heat and skim off any foam.

Using a ladle and a funnel, spoon hot mixture into prepared, sterile jars. Leave ¼ inch head space and remove air bubbles. Wipe the outer rim of the jars with a clean damp cloth to ensure a tight fit. Adjust the two-piece lids and secure snugly.

Place jars in hot water bath canner, making sure the water covers the jars by at least 1 inch. Boil for 10 minutes. Turn heat off, remove jars, and cool overnight. Remove outer lid and store.

Making Juice from Berries

To make any flavor jelly, the essential ingredient is juice. Below are simple directions to make natural juice from a variety of fresh berries.

To make juice from berries, first wash and stem the berries, then crush them by hand. Add ¼ to ½ cup of water to each quart of crushed berries and place this into a large stainless steel saucepan. Cover and simmer the mixture until the berries are soft. Strain the mixture through a damp jelly bag or cheesecloth. (The jelly bag or cheesecloth can be placed in a colander which can then be placed on top of a bowl. Allow the juice to drain slowly into the bowl.) Collect the juice in a bowl underneath the jelly bag (it may take 2 hours or even overnight).

Strawberry Jelly

Makes 5 half-pint jars

Ingredients:

3 ½ cups natural unsweetened strawberry juice
1 (1¾ oz.) package powdered pectin
4 ½ cups sugar

Directions:

Prepare jars, lids, and hot water bath canner according to manufacturer instructions.

Place strawberry juice in a large stainless steel saucepan and whisk in powdered pectin until dissolved. Bring mixture to a boil over high heat, stirring constantly. Add sugar and return mixture to a full rolling boil, stirring constantly. Continue the rolling boil for 1 minute. Remove from heat and skim off any foam.

Using a ladle and a funnel, spoon hot mixture into prepared, sterile jars. Leave ¼ inch head space and remove air bubbles. Wipe the outer rim of the jars with a clean damp cloth to ensure a tight fit. Adjust the two-piece lids and secure snugly.

Place jars in hot water bath canner, making sure the water covers the jars by at least 1 inch. Boil for 10 minutes. Turn heat off, remove jars, and cool overnight. Remove outer lid and store.

Apple and Peach Conserve

Ingredients:

2 cups apples, chopped
2 cups peaches, chopped
Juice of 2 lemons
3 cups sugar

Directions:

Use tart unpeeled apples and firm ripe peaches, cut into small pieces. Combine with lemon juice and sugar. Cook slowly until the apple is transparent (about 20 minutes). Pour into sterilized glass jars and seal.

Apple Preserves

Makes 6 half-pint jars

Ingredients:

6 cups apples, sliced, peeled, and cored
1 cup water
1 tablespoon lemon juice
1 (1¾ oz.) package powdered pectin
½ cup thinly sliced and seeded lemon
4 cups sugar
2 teaspoons nutmeg

Directions:

Prepare jars, lids, and hot water bath canner according to manufacturer instructions.

Place apples, water, and lemon juice in a large stainless steel saucepan. Bring mixture to a boil over high heat. Cover and simmer over low to medium heat for about 10 minutes, stirring occasionally. Remove mixture from the heat and whisk in powdered pectin until dissolved. Bring mixture to a boil over high heat, stirring constantly. Add lemon slices and sugar, stirring until sugar is dissolved. Return mixture to a full rolling boil, stirring constantly. Continue the rolling boil for 1 minute. Remove from heat and skim off any foam. Stir in nutmeg.

Using a ladle and a funnel, spoon hot mixture into prepared, sterile jars. Leave ¼ inch head space and remove air bubbles. Wipe the outer rim of the jars with a clean damp cloth to ensure a tight fit. Adjust the two-piece lids and secure snugly.

Place jars in hot water bath canner, making sure the water covers the jars by at least 1 inch. Boil for 15 minutes. Turn heat off, remove jars, and cool overnight. Remove outer lid and store.

Cherry Preserves

Makes 6 half-pint jars

Ingredients:

3 pounds pitted cherries
1 (1¾ oz.) package powdered pectin
5 cups sugar

Directions:

Prepare jars, lids, and hot water bath canner according to manufacturer instructions.

Combine cherries and powdered pectin in a large stainless steel saucepan. Bring mixture to a boil over high heat, stirring constantly. Add sugar and return mixture to a full rolling boil, stirring constantly. Continue the rolling boil for 1 minute. Remove from heat and skim off any foam. After removing from heat, stir for a few additional minutes to redistribute the fruit.

Using a ladle and a funnel, spoon hot mixture into prepared, sterile jars. Leave ¼ inch head space and remove air bubbles. Wipe the outer rim of the jars with a clean damp cloth to ensure a tight fit. Adjust the two-piece lids and secure snugly.

Place jars in hot water bath canner, making sure the water covers the jars by at least 1 inch. Boil for 15 minutes. Turn heat off, remove jars, and cool overnight. Remove outer lid and store.

HOME CANNING: HOME FRESHNESS

The benefits of home canning are tremendous. There is nothing better than being able to go into your own garden or to a local farmstand and gather the freshest produce available. There is no comparison in taste when comparing large factory farm produce to fresh-picked produce from a local farm or garden.

DESSERTS

Cake, cookies, pie, pudding, candy, pastries, ice cream… Dessert. The simply mention of that one word has the potential to cause mouths to salivate. Dessert, especially for those with a fondness for sweeter foods, is arguably a favorite part of any meal.

For many, holidays and special occasions simply wouldn't be complete without the presence of these sweet treats. In America, we commemorate birthdays with cake and ice cream, Thanksgiving with pumpkin and apple pie, and Christmas with cookies. We host ice cream socials and cake walks.

While it is sometimes assumed that desserts are inherently unhealthy, you'll find that many of the dessert recipes in this collection feature fruits and other natural ingredients to offer nutritional benefits while still being delicious. Tasty treats like Strawberry Shortcake (page 187) and Cranberry-Apple Pie (page 183) can be made from basic ingredients found in your kitchen, backyard garden, or local farmstand. Recipes such as the Maple Macadamia Nut Parfait (page 193) and Honey Apple Pudding (page 194) are also made with specialty items like pure maple syrup and pure honey that can be found at your local farmers market or farmstand.

Apple Strudel

Ingredients:

Apples, pared
Cinnamon and sugar, mixed
Butter, as needed
1 cup sugar

1 teaspoon baking powder
1 cup flour
½ teaspoon salt
1 egg

Directions:

Preheat the oven to 350°F. Into bottom of a buttered baking dish put thick layers of apples. Sprinkle with sugar and cinnamon mixed. Dot with lumps of butter. Into a mixing bowl sift the sugar, baking powder, flour, and salt. Into this break 1 egg. Mix until crumbly. Put over apples and bake for 30 minutes, or until crust is brown. Serve with milk, whipped cream or ice cream.

Apple Ring Fritters
Makes 16-20

Ingredients:

1 cup sifted flour
1½ teaspoons baking powder
2 tablespoons sugar
½ teaspoon salt
¾ cup milk
1 egg
4 large apples

Directions:

Sift dry ingredients. Add milk and egg. Beat well. Peel and core apples and slice in rings about ¼-inch thick. Dip rings in batter and drop into skillet containing ½-inch of hot melted shortening. Fry until golden brown on both sides. Drain on paper towel. Mix sugar and cinnamon together and sprinkle over fritters.

Maple Apple Squares

Courtesy of the New York State Maple Producers Association
(www.nysmaple.com)

Ingredients:

1 box yellow cake mix
1 stick butter
3-4 apples
1 (8 oz.) package sour cream
1 egg

¼ cup pure granulated maple sugar
1 teaspoon cinnamon
¼ cup pure maple syrup
Whipped cream

Directions:

In bowl, place yellow cake mix and butter (or margarine or butter substitute). Mix together with pastry blender until crumbly and reserve ⅔ cup in separate bowl. Pat the mixture into a 9- x 13-inch pan and top with thinly sliced apples. Mix together sour cream and egg, then spread over apples. Add maple sugar and cinnamon to the reserved ⅔ cup mixture and spread over the top of the sour cream layer. Bake at 350°F for 25 to 30 minutes. When cool, cut into squares and drizzle with maple syrup and a dollop of whipped cream.

Cranberry-Apple Pie

Ingredients:

1 pastry
2¼ cups sugar
½ cup water
2 cups apple slices
4 cups cranberries
2 tablespoons cornstarch
2 tablespoons water

Directions:

Roll out half of pastry and fit into 9-inch pie pan. Combine sugar, water, apple slices, and cranberries in saucepan. Cook until cranberries pop, about 10 minutes. Make a paste of cornstarch and remaining water, stir into fruit and continue cooking until thick and clear, about 5 minutes. Cool and pour into pie shell. Roll out remaining pastry and cut in strips. Arrange them in a crisscross fashion over top. Bake in 425°F oven for 25 minutes.

Honey Walnut Pumpkin Pie

Courtesy of the National Honey Board

(www.honey.com)

Ingredients:

3 eggs, slightly beaten
¾ cup honey
½ teaspoon ginger
½ teaspoon nutmeg
½ teaspoon cinnamon
½ teaspoon salt
1½ cups canned pumpkin
1 cup evaporated milk or half-and-half
1 9-inch unbaked pie shell

⅓ cup honey
⅓ cup chopped walnuts
¼ teaspoon vanilla

Honey whipped cream

1 cup whipping cream
3 tablespoons honey
1 teaspoon vanilla

Directions:

Combine all ingredients, except pie shell. Beat or blend until smooth. Pour into shell. Bake at 425°F for 10 minutes. Reduce oven temperature to 350°F. Bake for 35 to 40 minutes or until custard is set. Cool. Just before serving, combine ⅓ cup honey, ⅓ cup chopped walnuts and ¼ teaspoon vanilla. Carefully spread over top of pie. Serve with honey sweetened whipped cream.

Honey whipped cream

Beat whipping cream until mixture thickens; gradually add honey and beat until soft peaks form. Fold in vanilla. Makes 2 cups.

Maple Nut Fudge

Courtesy of the Massachusetts Maple Producers Association

(www.massmaple.org)

Ingredients:

2 cups sugar
1 cup pure maple syrup
2 tablespoons corn syrup
½ cup milk

1 teaspoon vanilla
1 cup chopped nuts
1 tablespoon butter

Directions:

Boil sugar, maple syrup, corn syrup, and milk, stirring constantly until 238°F. Remove from heat. Cool to 110°F. Add vanilla, nuts, and butter. Beat until thick and creamy. Pour into 8-inch pan and cut into squares when chilled.

Maple Lava Cakes

Courtesy of the New York State Maple Producers Association
(www.nysmaple.com)

Ingredients:

1½ cups sugar
½ cup butter
¼ cup pure maple syrup
2 eggs

½ cup milk
1¾ cups flour
½ teaspoon baking powder
¾ cup pure maple cream

Directions:

Preheat oven to 400°F. Butter 8 ramekins (medium custard cups). Beat together sugar and butter, then add the maple syrup. Add eggs one at a time. Add milk and mix well. In a separate bowl, mix the flour and baking powder, then add to batter and mix until smooth. Pour batter into the ramekins (about 6-7 tablespoons per cup). Put the ramekins on a cookie sheet and place in oven. Bake about 20 minutes or until the edges start to pull away. The centers will still be soft. Loosen the sides with a knife and turn upside down onto a dessert plate that is smeared with maple cream. Remove the ramekin. Finish with maple cream on the top of each cake and enjoy.

Apple Coffee Cake

Courtesy of NHLBI, part of NIH and HHS

Ingredients:

5 cups tart apples, cored, peeled, chopped
1 cup sugar
1 cup dark raisins
½ cup pecans, chopped
¼ cup vegetable oil

2 teaspoons vanilla
1 egg, beaten
1½ cups sifted all-purpose flour
1½ teaspoons baking soda
2 teaspoons ground cinnamon

Directions:

Preheat oven to 350°F. Lightly oil a 13- x 9- x 2-inch pan. In a large mixing bowl, combine apples with sugar, raisins, and pecans; mix well. Let stand 30 minutes. Stir in oil, vanilla, and egg. Sift together flour, baking soda, and cinnamon; stir into apple mixture about one-third at a time just enough to moisten dry ingredients. Turn batter into pan. Bake 35 to 40 minutes. Cool cake slightly before serving.

Note: Apples and raisins provide the moistness, which means less oil can be used in this low saturated fat, low cholesterol, and low-sodium coffee cake.

Maple Walnut Cream Cake

Ingredients:

⅓ cup butter
¾ cup sugar
1½ cups flour
2½ teaspoons baking powder

½ cup milk
1 teaspoon vanilla
2 egg whites
maple frosting, as needed
½ cup chopped walnuts

Directions:

Cream the butter and sugar. Mix and sift the flour with the baking powder, then add to the milk and vanilla. Beat thoroughly. Fold in egg whites, beaten stiff. Line and butter two to three round shallow pans. Bake in 350°F oven for 30-40 minutes or until toothpick inserted in center comes out clean (time may vary depending on the number and size of pans used). When cake is cooled, trim (if needed) and fill bottom layer with maple frosting and ½ cup small pieces of walnut. Place second cake on top and cover top and sides with maple frosting.

Blueberry Cake

Ingredients:

1 cup butter
2 cups powdered sugar
4 eggs, separated
3 cups flour
2 teaspoons baking powder

1 cup milk
1 teaspoon cinnamon, washed and floured
2 cups blueberries

Directions:

Cream the butter and powdered sugar together. Gradually add the yolks of all four eggs. Sift in the flour and baking powder. Add the milk, alternately with the flour, to the creamed mixture. Stir in the cinnamon and add stiff-beaten egg whites. Add the blueberries, which have been washed and rolled in flour. Be careful when stirring in the blueberries that you do not bruise them. Bake at 375°F for approximately 20 to 30 minutes.

Strawberry Shortcake

Ingredients:

Shortcake

2 cups flour
4 teaspoons baking powder
½ teaspoon salt
1 tablespoon sugar
¼ cup butter
¾ cup milk

Topping

1½ – 2 pints strawberries, cleaned and drained
Sugar, to taste

Directions:

Shortcake

Mix flour, baking powder, salt, and sugar. Work in butter and then add milk to the mixture. Toss the dough on a floured board, dividing in two parts. Pat, roll out, and place in two cake tins. Bake at 400°F for 12 minutes.

Topping

Meanwhile, hull and slice the strawberries. Sweeten them to taste with sugar. While the shortbread is still hot, spread butter on both layers. Crush the berries slightly and put them between and on top of the two layers of shortcake. Serve plain or with whipped cream.

Maple Cheesecake

Courtesy of Shaver-Hill Farm

(www.shaverhillfarm.com)

Ingredients:

1½ cups graham cracker crumbs
6 tablespoons sugar
⅓ cup melted butter or margarine
¾ cup pure maple syrup
¼ cup heavy cream

1½ pounds cream cheese, softened
3 eggs
1½ teaspoons vanilla
1½ cups sour cream

Directions:

Combine graham cracker crumbs, 2 tablespoons of sugar, and melted butter or margarine in a small mixing bowl and then press into the bottom of a 9-inch springform pan and freeze. Bring the maple syrup to a boil over medium heat in a saucepan. Boil three minutes, then remove from heat and stir in the heavy cream. Scrape into a bowl and refrigerate. Using an electric mixer, beat the cream cheese until light and fluffy. Add the remaining 4 tablespoons of sugar and beat briefly, then add the eggs. When the maple syrup is no longer warm to the touch, gradually beat it in, followed by the vanilla and sour cream. Spread the filling mixture into the chilled pan and bake for 1 hour. Transfer to a rack and thoroughly cool. Cover and chill at least 6 hours before serving.

Velvety Pumpkin Cheesecake

Courtesy of John Scheepers Kitchen Garden Seeds

(www.kitchengardenseeds.com)

Ingredients:

Crust

1 teaspoon cinnamon

¼ cup sugar

¼ cup melted unsalted butter

1½ cups crushed ginger snap cookies

Filling

1 pound cream cheese (at room temperature)

3 eggs

1 cup sugar

1 pound ricotta cheese

1 cup sour cream

1 cup cooked, pureed pumpkin flesh

2 teaspoons vanilla

3 tablespoons cornstarch

Pinch of salt

Directions:

Crust

Preheat oven to 350°F. Mix crust ingredients together and spread in bottom of a 10-inch greased springform cake pan.

Filling

In large mixing bowl, beat the cream cheese until smooth. Add the eggs, one at a time, beating until smooth. Add sugar slowly and mix until fluffy. Add ricotta cheese, sour cream, and pureed pumpkin and mix until smooth. Add vanilla, cornstarch, and salt and mix to blend. Pour mixture over crust. Bake at 350°F for one hour. Turn oven off and leave cheesecake in closed oven for another hour. Remove from oven and let cool to room temperature. Refrigerate. Remove from springform pan. Lovely with freshly whipped cream sweetened with a bit of brown sugar.

Note: You can vary the degree of pumpkin flavor: the total contribution of the pumpkin and sour cream should be two cups however you divide it.

Rolled Maple Sugar Cookies

Courtesy of the New York State Maple Producers Association

(www.nysmaple.com)

Makes 6 dozen 3-inch cookies

Ingredients:

1 cup shortening

¾ cup pure maple sugar

1 cup white sugar

2 eggs, well beaten

2 tablespoons milk

2 teaspoons vanilla

4 cups flour

2 teaspoons baking powder

½ teaspoon salt

Directions:

Cream shortening with sugars. Add well-beaten eggs, milk and vanilla. Add flour, baking powder, and salt, sifted together. Mix and chill thoroughly. Roll out thin on floured board and cut with cookie cutter. Bake on greased cookie sheets in 350°F oven for 10 minutes.

Maple Oatmeal Cookies

Courtesy of Shaver-Hill Farm

(www.shaverhillfarm.com)

Ingredients:

1½ cups butter

1¾ cups pure maple syrup

1 cup granulated sugar

2 eggs

2 teaspoons vanilla

6 cups oats, uncooked

2 cups all-purpose flour

1 teaspoon salt

2 teaspoons baking soda

Directions:

Preheat oven to 350°F. Beat together butter, syrup, sugar, eggs and vanilla. Add oats. Mix together and add flour, salt and baking soda. Mix well. Drop by rounded teaspoonfuls onto greased cookie sheet. Bake for 12 to 15 minutes.

Note: For variety, add ½ cup of any or all of the following: chopped nuts, raisins, chocolate chips or coconut.

Pumpkin Cookies

Contributed by Chef Nancy Berkoff, The Vegetarian Resource Group, Vegetarian Journal
(www.vrg.org)
Makes approximately 48 cookies

Ingredients:

1 cup non-hydrogenated vegan margarine
1 cup sugar (use your favorite vegan variety)
1 cup canned or cooked pumpkin
3 tablespoons mashed banana
1 teaspoon vanilla extract
2 cups unbleached flour
1 teaspoon baking powder

1 teaspoon cinnamon
1 teaspoon ground ginger
½ teaspoon cloves
½ teaspoon allspice
½ cup chopped raisins
½ cup chopped dates
Vegetable oil spray

Directions:

Preheat oven to 375°F. Spray a baking sheet with oil. In a large bowl, combine margarine and sugar until well mixed. Add pumpkin, banana, and vanilla and stir to combine. In a separate bowl, mix together the flour, baking powder, and spices. Add to pumpkin mixture and stir. Mix in raisins and dates. Drop by teaspoonfuls onto the baking sheet. Bake cookies for 15 minutes or until just crisp on the edges.

Note: Do not overbake these cookies, as they can be rather dry. These go well with hot or cold tea, milk, or coffee. The cookies can also be crumbled over cooked hot cereal.

Maple Bavarian Cream

Ingredients:

4 eggs, separated
1 cup pure maple syrup
Pinch salt
1 package gelatin
2 tablespoons cold water
½ pint cream

Directions:

Boil egg yolks, maple syrup, and salt in a double boiler until it reaches the consistency of custard. Stir while cooking. Soak gelatin in the water. Add to the maple syrup mixture while still hot. Let cool. Beat the egg whites until stiff and combine with the mixture. Add the cream. Place in a mold to cool.

Honey Taffy

Courtesy of Bees-And-Beekeeping.com

Ingredients:
2 cups sugar
¾ cup honey

1 cup water
2 tablespoons butter

Directions:
Combine the sugar, honey, and water in a saucepan and cook until it reaches 278°F or until the soft-crack stage. (The soft-crack stage is when a bit of the syrup is dropped into cold water and it forms solid threads that are flexible, not brittle. The threads can be bent slightly without breaking.) While heating the mixture, stir constantly until the sugar is dissolved, and then stir occasionally to prevent scorching. Remove from heat and stir in the butter. Stir as little as possible, only enough to mix in the butter. Pour the candy into greased pans and allow to cool until it is safe to handle with bare hands. Gather the taffy into a ball and pull it repeatedly until it becomes somewhat firm and light in color. Stretch the taffy out into a long rope and cut into bite-sized pieces with a pair of scissors. Wrap each piece of taffy in waxed paper.

Awesome Honey Pecan Pie

Courtesy of Benefits of Honey, the number one ranked website
on the health benefits of honey
(www.benefits-of-honey.com)

Ingredients:
¼ pound butter
1 cup sugar
3 eggs, beaten
½ cup corn syrup
½ cup honey
½ teaspoon vanilla
½ teaspoon lemon juice

1-2 cups chopped or whole pecans
1 pinch cinnamon
1 pinch nutmeg (optional, for a more exotic aroma)
9-inch uncooked pie shell

Directions:
Preheat oven to 325°F. In a heavy-bottomed saucepan, brown butter over medium-high heat to get a nice nutty aroma for the pie (be careful not to burn it). Remove and allow to cool slightly. In a large mixing bowl combine sugar, eggs, syrup, and honey. Using a wire whisk, blend all ingredients well. Add the browned butter, vanilla, lemon juice, and pecans. Season with cinnamon and nutmeg. Continue to whip until all ingredients are well blended. Pour into pie shell and bake on center rack of oven for 45 minutes to an hour. Remove and allow to cool before serving.

Pumpkin Crème Caramel

Courtesy of John Scheepers Kitchen Garden Seeds

(www.kitchengardenseeds.com)

There is nothing better than savoring the goodness of homegrown vegetables and herbs through winter's cold, dark months. Like serving my own pesto bubbling atop warm goat cheese with crackers, or sneaking into the freezer for my choice of herbed butters, or serving my pumpkin crème caramel on Thanksgiving.

Ingredients:

1 cup sugar

1 cup heavy cream

1 cup milk

1 tablespoon vanilla paste

3 eggs

2 egg yolks

½ cup sugar

½ cup cooked pumpkin puree

Pinch of ground cloves, cinnamon and nutmeg (optional)

Directions:

Pour one cup of sugar into a heavy skillet. Slowly melt the sugar until it is a smooth, golden caramel. Pour the caramel into a 1½ quart soufflé dish, swirling it around to cover the bottom and three inches up the sides. Place the soufflé dish in a baking pan of cold water. Combine the heavy cream, milk and vanilla paste in a saucepan. Heat to scalding and simmer for 8 minutes. In a large bowl, whip the eggs and egg yolks until frothy. Slowly add ½ cup sugar, blending well. Add the cooked pumpkin puree, beating until well incorporated and smooth.

Add ever so small pinches of ground cloves, cinnamon, and nutmeg if preferred. In a steady stream, pour the hot cream mixture into the egg mixture while whisking. Pour the custard into the soufflé dish. Bake at 350°F for one hour. Let it cool. Once cool, invert the crème caramel onto a larger plate with sides to catch the delicious caramel. Serve with a dollop of freshly whipped cream sweetened with brown sugar and a hint of vanilla.

Note: To make cooked pumpkin puree, select a beautiful Rouge d'Etampes, Spookacular or Long Island Cheese pumpkin. Each pound produces about one cup of puree. Cut the pumpkin in half and scoop out the seeds and fibers. Wipe the surface with a paper towel dipped in canola oil. Place the pumpkin halves on a baking sheet, fill with about an inch of water and cover with foil. Bake in a preheated 350°F oven for 60 to 90 minutes or until the pumpkin flesh is soft and tender when pierced with a knife.

Maple Macadamia Nut Parfait

Courtesy of the New York State Maple Producers Association

(www.nysmaple.com)

Serves 4

Ingredients:

1 package Knox® gelatin
1 cup cold water
1 cup pure maple syrup
Macadamia nuts or other available nuts

Directions:

Soak gelatin in ¼ cup cold water for 5 minutes. Bring syrup to boil. Stir in gelatin and stir until clear. Add remaining cold water. Stir. Refrigerate (this may take 2 to 3 hours, depending upon how cold the water used is). When mixture is almost set, beat until fluffy. Put in glasses, then into refrigerator until ready to serve. When serving, decorate with whipped cream, nuts, or cherries as desired.

Note: This dish may also be prepared the day before and simply garnished with desired toppings when ready to serve.

Café Parfait

Ingredients:

1 pint cream
4 egg yolks
6 ounces sugar
4 ounces coffee beans
1 cup strong coffee
Maraschino liqueur, to taste (optional)

Directions:

Put the cream, egg yolks, and sugar on stove and whip until it begins to thicken. Add beans and coffee. Let stand for one hour or more. Place in freezer until stiff, then add an additional pint of thick cream and maraschino liqueur (optional) to taste.

Honey Apple Pudding

Courtesy of Bees-And-Beekeeping.com

Ingredients:

2 cups stewed apples
1 cup honey
½ cup brown sugar
4 tablespoons shortening
2 cups fine bread crumbs

1½ cups flour
2 tablespoons baking powder
2 teaspoons cinnamon
½ teaspoon cloves

Directions:

Combine all ingredients and beat until thoroughly mixed. Pour into a baking dish and bake for 35 minutes at 300°F. Serve the pudding with a thin applesauce that has been sweetened with honey.

Blackberry Pudding

Ingredients:

1 cup flour
1½ cups fine bread crumbs
½ teaspoon salt
1 tablespoon baking powder
1 egg

1½ cups water
2 cups blackberries, washed
¼ teaspoon nutmeg

Directions:

Add all ingredients in a large bowl and mix well. Pour into a pudding dish and bake on 350°F for about 45 minutes.

Honey Pumpkin Mousse

Courtesy of the National Honey Board

(www.honey.com)

Ingredients:

4 eggs, separated
¾ cup honey
16 ounces fresh pumpkin puree
2 tablespoons all-purpose flour
1½ teaspoons ground cinnamon

½ teaspoon ground ginger
¼ teaspoon ground nutmeg
¼ teaspoon salt

Directions:

In top of double boiler, combine egg whites and honey. Cook over simmering water, stirring constantly, until mixture reaches 160°F; transfer mixture to a medium bowl. Using electric mixer on high speed, beat egg whites until cool and glossy peaks form; set aside. In medium saucepan, combine egg yolks, pumpkin, flour, cinnamon, ginger, nutmeg and salt. Cook over medium heat, stirring constantly, until mixture boils; remove from heat. Gently stir 1/4 of beaten egg whites into pumpkin mixture; gradually fold remaining egg whites into lightened mixture. Spoon mousse into dessert glasses; cover and chill.

Plum-Raspberry Dessert Soup

Ingredients:

8 medium-sized fresh plums (1½ lbs.)
1 cup fresh or frozen raspberries
3 (3 inch) cinnamon sticks
1½ cups red dinner wine
1 tablespoon corn starch

2 tablespoons sugar
Low-fat frozen yogurt, for garnish
Mint, for garnish (optional)

Directions:

Combine plums, berries, cinnamon, and red wine in saucepan. Bring to a boil, then reduce heat and simmer for 15 minutes. Whisk cornstarch with ½ cup water. Add to soup and cook, stirring until thickened. Add sugar to taste. Cool. Discard cinnamon then puree in electric blender. Chill until ready to serve. To serve, portion soup into shallow bowls. Add small scoop of low-fat frozen yogurt to the center of each bowl and garnish with mint, if desired.

DESSERTS

Maple Baked Pears

Courtesy of the New York State Maple Producers Association

(www.nysmaple.com)

Ingredients:

2 ripe but firm Bartlett pears
4 tablespoons lemon juice
1 tablespoon unsalted butter
2 tablespoons pure granulated maple sugar

2 tablespoons pure maple syrup (or more to taste)
½ teaspoon pure vanilla extract
Water (optional)

Directions:

Preheat oven to 375°F. Peel the pears and cut them in half lengthwise. Using a melon baller or a spoon, scoop out the cores. Brush the pears with lemon juice to prevent browning. Melt the butter in an oven proof skillet just large enough to hold the pears in a single layer. Add the granulated maple sugar and cook over moderately low heat, stirring, until the sugar is dissolved. Add the pears and turn them several times to coat with the syrup. Arrange the pears, cut side down, in a single layer and bake for about 30 minutes, basting occasionally with pan juices, until just softened and golden. Transfer the pears to a platter and keep warm. If necessary, add a little water to the skillet to thin the syrup. Remove from the heat and stir in the vanilla. Pour the syrup over the pears and serve warm or at room temperature.

Banana-Apple Sherbet

Ingredients:

2 large ripe bananas
1 tablespoon fresh lemon juice
1½ cups fresh applesauce
3 tablespoons honey

Directions:

Cut the bananas into 1-inch-thick slices; dip in the lemon juice to prevent browning. Arrange the bananas on a baking sheet. Place in the freezer for about 4 hours, or until firm. Pour the applesauce into an ice cube tray. Place in the freezer for about 4 hours, or until firm. In a food processor or blender, combine the frozen bananas and applesauce and purée until almost smooth. Add the honey and process until smooth and creamy. Scoop into serving dishes and serve immediately.

Cranberry Sherbet
Makes 1 quart

Ingredients:
4 cups cranberries
2¾ cups water
2 cups sugar
1 tablespoon gelatin (1 envelope)
¼ cup cold water
Juice and grated rind 1 lemon
Juice and grated rind 1 orange

Directions:
Combine cranberries, water, and sugar in saucepan. Cook until cranberries are soft. Put through sieve or food mill. Soften gelatin in cold water and dissolve in hot cranberry puree. Stir in fruit juice and rind. Cool. Pour into refrigerator tray and freeze until firm.

Mango Sorbet
Serves 4

Ingredients:
2 medium mangos, peeled and cubed
2 teaspoons sugar
¾ cup yogurt

Directions:
In food processor, process mango and sugar until smooth. Add yogurt. Pour mixture into freezer container of an ice cream maker. Freeze according to manufacturer's instructions. To prepare without an ice cream maker, pour mixture into an 8- x 4-inch freezer container. Cover and freeze 4 hours, whisking from time to time.

Vanilla Ice Cream

Ingredients:

3½ quarts milk
3 cups sugar
¾ cup flour
¾ teaspoon salt

6 eggs
3 tablespoons vanilla
1 quart heavy cream

Directions:

Scald milk in a double boiler. Mix sugar, flour, and salt together, adding milk gradually. Return to a double boiler. Cook for 20 minutes, stirring constantly until smooth. Add slightly beaten eggs, cook for three minutes, and cool. Add flavoring and cream, then freeze.

Strawberry Honey Ice Cream

Courtesy of the American Beekeeping Federation (ABF)

(www.abfnet.org)

Ingredients:

4 eggs
2¼ cups honey
4 cups milk
2 cups heavy cream
2 cups evaporated milk
1 teaspoon salt
2 tablespoons vanilla

2 cups crushed strawberries
A few whole strawberries, for garnish
Fresh mint, for garnish

Directions:

In a large mixing bowl, beat eggs until uniform and gradually add honey, mixing well. Add milk, cream, evaporated milk, salt, and vanilla. Mix all ingredients together. Put in ice cream freezer and once cream is firm (or after about 15 minutes), add crushed strawberries. Continue to freeze ice cream until firm. Put in container and set in freezer for three or four hours. Serve with a fresh strawberry and a sprig of mint to finish.

RESOURCES

We would like to thank the following organizations who have shared their delicious recipes for inclusion in this collection. Please visit their websites for more information.

American Beekeeping Federation
www.abfnet.org

American Grassfed Association
www.americangrassfed.org

American Institute for Cancer Research
www.aicr.org

Bees-And-Beekeeping.com
www.bees-and-beekeeping.com

Benefits of Honey
www.benefits-of-honey.com

British Tomato Growers' Association
www.britishtomatoes.co.uk

Cape Cod Cranberry Growers' Association
www.cranberries.org

Central New York Tomatofest
www.cnytomatofest.org

Champagne® Mango
www.champagnemango.com

Cornerstone Garlic Farm
www.localharvest.org/cornerstone-garlic-farm-M6792

Florida Tomato Committee
www.floridatomatoes.org

Garelick Farms
www.garelickfarms.com

Garlic Seed Foundation
www.garlicseedfoundation.info

Greensgrow Farm
www.greensgrow.org

Health Benefits of Honey
www.health-benefi ts-of-honey.com

Hood River Garlic Farm
www.hoodrivergarlic.com

I Love Eggplant!
www.iloveeggplant.com

John Scheepers Kitchen Garden Seeds
www.kitchengardenseeds.com

Mariquita Farm
www.mariquita.com

Massachusetts Maple Producers' Association
www.massmaple.org

Mt. Vikos
www.mtvikos.com

National Dairy Council
www.nationaldairycouncil.org

National Honey Board
www.honey.com

National Pasta Association
www.ilovepasta.org

New York State Maple Producers Association
www.nysmaple.com

Red Fire Farm
www.redfirefarm.com

Shaver-Hill Farm
www.shaverhillfarm.com

Toronto Garlic Festival
www.torontogarlicfestival.ca

Tropical Cheese Industries
www.tropicalcheese.com

Vegetarian Resource Group
www.vrg.org

World's Healthiest Foods
www.whfoods.com

INDEX

Grape Kabobs with Yogurt, 103
Greek Potato Salad with Feta Cheese, 47
Grilled Steak with Pumpkin Puree, 83
Grilled Tofu Kabobs with Chipotle Marinade, 101

H
Harvest Pumpkin Muffins, 8
Hearty Pumpkin Soup, 30
Homemade Black Beans, 119
Homemade Granola with Pumpkin Yogurt, 10
Honey
> A Honey of a Chili, 105
> Apple-Honey Oatmeal, 9
> Awesome Honey Pecan Pie, 191
> Celery and Apple Steam-Fry with Honey Mustard Sauce, 96
> Chicken Chili, 78
> Cinnamon Flavor Honey Butter, 171
> Cornmeal Pancakes with Honey Fruit Sauce, 4
> Curried Date Carrot Soup, 37
> Exotic Grilled Honey Wings, 79
> Fruit and Nuts Honey Butter, 172
> Fruit Soup, 39
> Grilled Tofu Kabobs with Chipotle Marinade, 101
> Honey Apple Pudding, 194
> Honey Apricot Bread, 148
> Honey Bourbon Chicken, 79
> Honey Bran Muffins, 7
> Honey Candied Sweet Potatoes, 131
> Honey Chinese BBQ Pork, 88
> Honey French Toast, 6
> Honey Glazed Salmon, 62
> Honey Mustard Dressing, 160
> Honey Pumpkin Mousse, 195
> Honey Pumpkin Tea Bread, 152
> Honey Punch, 135
> Honey Sweet and Sour Meatballs, 82
> Honey Taffy, 191
> Honey Walnut Pumpkin Pie, 184
> Honey Walnut Shrimp, 65
> Honey Whole-Wheat Bread, 149
> Honey-Mustard Salmon, 62
> Hot Honey Cider, 137
> Kiddy Fruity Honey Smoothie, 143

Roasted Chicken with Pumpkin Risotto, 76
Roasted Pumpkin Seeds, 117
Seared Scallops with Pumpkin Timbale, 67
Shrimp with Pumpkin and Zucchini Fettuccini, 68
Stewed Pumpkin with Tomatoes, 99
Velvety Pumpkin Cheesecake, 188
Purifier Smoothie, 143

Q
Quick Spinach Casserole, 105
Quinoa and Pumpkin Seeds Salad, 50

R
Rainbow Fruit Salad, 54
Raspberry
      Plum-Raspberry Dessert Soup, 195
      Raspberry Punch, 134
      Red Cooler, 139
Roast Pork Loin with Apples and Cinnamon, 85
Roast Turkey with Honey Cranberry Relish, 80
Roasted Acorn Squash and Apple Soup, 28
Roasted Chicken Legs with Jalapeño and Tomato, 77
Roasted Chicken with Pumpkin Risotto, 76
Roasted Duck with Currant Jelly Sauce, 91
Roasted Garlic and Winter Vegetables, 97
Roasted Garlic Grilled Cheese Sandwich, 104
Roasted Garlic Soup with Thyme Croutons, 32
Roasted Garlic Spread with Sweet or Savory Toppings, 169
Roasted Pumpkin Seeds, 117
Roasted Tomato Soup, 35
Rolled Maple Sugar Cookies, 189
Rosemary Potato Skewers, 122

S
Salads
      Apple, Date and Orange Salad, 54
      Artichoke and Roasted Red Pepper Salad with Red Pepper Dressing, 53
      Asian Apple-Chicken Salad, 44
      Beets and Pumpkin Salad, 49
      Cold Pasta Salad with Char-Grilled Tomato Sauce, 45
      Curly Endive with Bacon and Pumpkin, 45
      Dilled Granny Apple Chicken Salad, 44
      Fruit and Pumpkin Salad, 55

Also in the *Farmstand Favorites* Series:

Farmstand Favorites: Apples
978-1-57826-358-5

Farmstand Favorites: Berries
978-1-57826-375-2

Farmstand Favorites: Canning & Preserving
978-1-57826-415-5

Farmstand Favorites: Cheese & Dairy
978-1-57826-395-0

Farmstand Favorites: Garlic
978-1-57826-405-6

Farmstand Favorites: Honey
978-1-57826-406-3

Farmstand Favorites: Maple Syrup
978-1-57826-369-1

Farmstand Favorites: Pumpkins
978-1-57826-357-8

Farmstand Favorites: Tomatoes
978-1-57826-411-7

My Recipes

My Recipes

My Recipes

My Recipes

My Recipes

My Recipes

My Recipes

My Recipes

My Recipes

My Recipes